FIREFIGHTER

career starter

2nd edition

Mary Masi
with Lauren B. Starkey

LEARNINGEXPRESS

New York

Copyright © 2001 LearningExpress, LLC.

All rights reserved under International and Pan-American Copyright Conventions.
Published in the United States by LearningExpress, LLC, New York.

Library of Congress Cataloging-in-Publication Data:
Masi, Mary.
    Firefighter career starter / Mary Masi, with Lauren Starkey.
        p. cm.
    ISBN -57685-365-9 (pbk.)
    1. Fire extinction—Vocational guidance—United States. I. Starkey, Lauren B., 1962–
    II.Title.

TH9119 .M37 2001
363.37'023—dc21   00-051845

Printed in the United States of America
9 8 7 6 5 4 3 2
Second Edition

Regarding the Information in this Book

Every effort has been made to ensure the accuracy of directory information up until press time. However, phone numbers and/or addresses are subject to change. Please contact the respective organization for the most recent information.

For Further Information

For information on LearningExpress, other LearningExpress products, or bulk sales, please write to us at:

LearningExpress™
900 Broadway
Suite 604
New York, NY 10003

Or visit our website at:
www.learnatest.com

Contents

CONTENTS

Introduction

Why You Need This Book

THE BUREAU of Labor Statistics reports that there were over 314,000 paid, full-time career firefighters working in the United States in 1998. That number doesn't include an estimated one million volunteer and on-call firefighters. They project that the need for more firefighters will grow through 2005 as the increasing population demands increasing fire protection. But just because the fire protection field requires a larger labor force, don't expect to sail into your first job without working hard to attain it.

Firefighting is a highly sought-after career. Because so many people want to work in the fire protection field, numerous candidates apply for each job opening. Expect stiff competition from these candidates. Although the minimum educational requirement in most cities and states is a high school diploma or GED (general equivalency diploma), anticipate that many of those competing with you for the same job(s) will have completed training courses. This advanced education includes certificate programs, which take weeks or months to complete, through college degrees, which require a commitment of a number of years.

You can increase your chances of landing a job in fire protection by reading this book and applying what you've learned to your job search. Not only will you learn about the various training courses available, but you'll see where to find them and how to pay for them as well. Other subjects covered include the complicated job application process, different types of jobs available in the field, and how to succeed once you've landed a job. Throughout the book, you will get helpful information from those already working in the field.

In Chapter 1, you'll get an inside look at the best opportunities in firefighting today, from municipal firefighter to fire inspector to federal, state, and private job possibilities. This chapter contains specific job descriptions, typical salaries, and minimum requirements for those jobs. We also cover trends in the education available to prospective and working firefighters. If you are willing to relocate to land the job you want, you'll find information about the fastest-growing fire departments in the country.

Chapter 2 shows you how to land a job in the fire service field. First, you'll read about the qualities possessed by the candidates who get hired. There is detailed information on every step of the application process for a range of positions, including how to prepare for the written and physical exams and how to ace oral interviews. No job search today is complete without the Internet, so we've provided tips for using it as well as many Websites that can get your search started right away.

In Chapter 3, the education you'll need for your future career is explored, beginning with high school and the volunteer training available to teens. We'll explain the training courses offered beyond the high school level and provide actual degree requirements for fire science programs. These course descriptions can help you decide what training program is right for you and how long your schooling will last for each. You'll also find a directory of fire science training programs across the country in Appendix D.

After you've determined the education you need, Chapter 4 will explain the various ways with which to finance it. The general types of financial aid are explained, and the application process is broken down into easy-to-follow steps. You will even learn the largest sources of aid and where to look for more. Other helpful information includes glossaries of financial aid terms and acronyms.

Once you've completed your training program and landed your first job, Chapter 5 shows you how to succeed on that job. You'll be taken through the first days as a probationary firefighter through to advancement opportunities. The promotion process is explained, with job descriptions and sample job postings for advanced positions. Finally, you'll learn about other career options within the fire protection field.

Good luck with your job search and new career!

FIREFIGHTER CAREER STARTER

CHAPTER one

CHOOSING A CAREER IN FIREFIGHTING

THIS CHAPTER is a report on the current state of the firefighting field. You'll learn about the benefits of the job as well as emerging educational trends for prospective firefighters around the country. Job descriptions, requirements, and salaries are listed for the following entry-level positions: municipal and volunteer firefighters, state and federal wildland firefighters, military and private company firefighters, EMT (emergency medical technician) firefighters, fire inspectors, and fire protection engineers. The chapter ends with a quiz that may help you to find out if you're suited for this exciting career.

THE NATURE of firefighting has changed dramatically from the days when firefighters only responded to fires. Today, many firefighters are certified as EMTs or paramedics to meet the increasing need for such services. Many calls to the firehouse require emergency procedures unrelated to fires, such as providing help to a heart attack victim or dealing with hazardous materials. Firefighters also respond to vehicle accidents, vehicle fires, terrorist attacks, earthquakes, hurricanes and other natural disasters, and many miscellaneous 911 emergency calls. Therefore they need a broad range of skills, and they need to continually update their skills by receiving additional training. As new technologies and equipment are created and responses to emergencies and disasters change in scope, the demands on firefighters will become increasingly complex. However, along with all those demands come many benefits that firefighters receive while in the line of duty.

ADVANTAGES OF BECOMING A FIREFIGHTER

Men and women are attracted to the firefighting field for a variety of reasons. Some seek the adventure and excitement, while others like the stability of a profession with good benefits, a salary that increases with years of service, and a great retirement plan. Firefighters are also perceived well by the public, and many job candidates like the fact that, once hired, they will be looked upon as heroes. Below, we look closely at some of the best aspects of the job.

Work Schedule

Firefighting is not a profession in which you'll end up behind a desk, working nine to five for five days a week. The variety of the work schedule appeals to people who want flexibility and large chunks of time off from work. Some firefighters even use their days off to earn side income, supplementing their firefighting salary. The average number of hours firefighters work each week is in the range of 42–52. Some of those hours, however, are spent in the firehouse, eating, sleeping, or relaxing.

In addition to waiting for calls, shifts involve firefighters engaging in a wide range of tasks, including maintenance of equipment and training, and may be followed by free time to relax. Schedules vary from department to department, but commonly firefighters work for 24 hours on duty followed by 48 or even 72 hours off duty. In large urban fire departments, each shift may be shorter, such as 8 to 14 hours, depending on if it is a day, night, or weekend shift.

The Lure of Adventure

While firefighting is dangerous and demanding work, several people say they joined the profession because they enjoy the excitement and rush of adrenaline that accompany fire calls. Each call can be different, and there is no way to predict the types of crises that will be met on each shift. Some firefighters jump out of airplanes to fight wildland fires, others scout out dangerous areas inside structures. Many firefighters save people's lives and property on a regular basis. They face danger and unknown conditions every time they go out on an emergency call.

Teamwork and Family Atmosphere

Since firefighters live and work so closely with each other, they often develop close bonds. Teamwork is essential in fighting fires and is emphasized from day one in all training programs. This teamwork provides a secure atmosphere for all the members of the team. Firefighters spend a great deal of time with each other when on long shifts at the firehouse; they often cook and eat large family-style meals around a big table and relax together when not out on calls. They take training courses together and test their skills by performing drills in friendly competition with each other. Kevin Scarbrough of the Ann Arbor, Michigan, fire department says firefighters sometimes play practical jokes on each other while in the firehouse to help relieve the buildup of tension from the underlying feeling of danger that accompanies most fire calls. The joking may also "test" how people will react to the group when in a fire situation.

Positive Public Perception

Although not all firefighters will admit it, most enjoy being perceived as heroes by the public. Many children look up to firefighters with awe and respect, often citing the profession as the one they want when they grow up. Even among adults, firefighters are often treated with a great deal of respect due to the dangerous and heroic nature of their job. Not only do they save people's lives and property, but they also provide emergency assistance in natural disasters and other times of calamity.

Health, Life, and Disability Insurance Benefits

Firefighters usually have a choice of health plans (medical and dental) to select from their employer. These plans cover the firefighter and his or her dependents. Life and disability insurance is also provided. If firefighters are injured on the job, they can either get disability payments or retire early, depending on the nature of the injury and the department's guidelines. Indeed, most states require that all local fire departments offer disability retirement benefits to their firefighters.

Retirement Benefits

Firefighters normally receive excellent retirement benefits and retire earlier than those employed in other professions. Due to the arduous nature of the job, many firefighters retire as soon as they reach the eligible age or time on the job. For example, some firefighters need to work for 25 years or until they are 55 years old, whichever comes first. If you became a firefighter when you were 20 years old, you could retire at age 45. However, some departments require you to work until age 55, regardless of your age when you were hired (meaning that it is possible to retire, with benefits, after serving much less than 20 years).

As with many other jobs, firefighters can set aside a portion of their paycheck every month without paying tax on the money until they use it during retirement. This type of pension plan, often called a deferred compensation plan, also allows you to choose how the money is invested. Many fire departments will contribute to your pension plan, meaning that money you haven't earned or saved will be earning interest and waiting for you when you retire.

Good Salary

The earnings of firefighters are high compared to other jobs requiring a similar amount of training. Typically, entry-level firefighters earn a significant salary, which then increases with experience and additional training. Most fire departments offer firefighters longevity pay after they've served a number of years. Longevity pay is a set amount added to firefighters' base salary every year after they become eligible to receive it. For instance, in the San Antonio, Texas, fire department, base pay increases by 3% for each 5 years of employment, up to 18% for 30 years.

Later in this chapter, you will find recent salary information for a number of jobs involving fire suppression and fire prevention. Many firefighters are also offered voluntary overtime on a rotating basis. Overtime offers a chance to significantly increase your salary, but it is an option that can also be rejected if the extra hours on the job aren't wanted. The only exception is when departments occasionally require mandatory overtime, such as in the case of a severe forest fire season.

Access to a Union

Many firefighters belong to unions, either on a national or a local level. These unions represent the needs of their members by working for passage of laws and safety regulations, establishing training programs, and maintaining standards for the industry. The largest firefighter's labor organization in the country is the International Association of Fire Fighters (IAFF), which has approximately 225,000 members. Some states have their own organizations. In California, the California State Firefighter's Association (CSFA) has been around for over 70 years and boasts over 28,000 members. The CSFA uses its resources to negotiate better wages and benefits and fair personnel policies for its members. It also offers its members additional life, health, disability, group, and long-term care insurance.

JUST THE FACTS

The International Association of Fire Fighters is one of the oldest public employee unions in the country. It was formed in 1918, when firefighters were required to live in firehouses on 24-hour duty. There were very few civil service laws to protect public employees, so firefighters were at the mercy of local departments when it came to pay, promotions to better jobs, and benefits. The IAFF has worked to change those conditions, as well as to promote health and safety regulations for its members.

Miscellaneous Benefits

Other benefits commonly given to municipal firefighters include paid vacations, holidays, and sick time; a uniform allowance for laundry and purchase of new uniforms; free training programs and tuition assistance for college and university fire studies; sick leave accrual; a free annual medical examination; and physical-conditioning training and equipment to work on.

EDUCATIONAL TRENDS

While the published entrance requirements for becoming a municipal career firefighter are minimal, more and more applicants are gaining training and certification to boost their chances of getting hired. And fire departments are beginning to seek candidates who have continued their education beyond high school. As the demands on firefighters' skills increase, so does the demand for their education and training. The Houston, Texas, fire department requires 60 hours of college credit as of September 1, 1999. Years ago, firefighters could easily get hired with only the minimum requirements (having a high school diploma and being at least 18 years of age). However, in response to stiff competition for a limited number of jobs, serious applicants are now taking advantage of many training programs and coming to the job with at least some college credit.

Many prospective firefighters enroll in fire science certificate or associate degree programs or take specific courses such as Fire Hose and Fire Streams, Fire Behavior, Fire Tools and Equipment, and other fire-related courses to attain basic fire-fighting skills. Other prospective firefighters also complete associate in science (AS) degrees or obtain certificates from local colleges in Emergency Medical Technology to increase their chances of landing a fire-fighting job.

To become the most attractive job candidate, you should consider education beyond high school. If you are in a medium to large city, chances are that some other applicants have or are attaining EMT, paramedic, or fire science training. Twenty-five years ago, when you were hired by a fire department, you were put through 12 to 16 weeks of training courses. Now, in cities like Miami, training takes six months. See Chapter 3 for more detailed information about the types of training programs that are available and how to choose the one that's best for you.

WHO EMPLOYS FIREFIGHTERS?

Over 314,000 career firefighters were employed nationwide as paid, full-time professionals in 1998, according to the Bureau of Labor Statistics. Where are these career firefighters employed? More than nine out of 10 of them work for municipal or county fire departments, typically serving communities with populations of 50,000 or more. Not surprisingly, bigger cities are the largest employers.

Full-time firefighters are also hired by federal and state government agencies to protect government-owned property and special facilities. For example, the U.S. Forest Service, Bureau of Land Management, and Park Service offer both year-round and seasonal fire service jobs to protect the country's national parks, forests and other lands.

In the private sector, many large industrial companies have their own fire-fighting forces, especially companies in the oil, chemical, aircraft, and aerospace industries. Other employers include airports, shipyards, and military bases. Also, a growing number of private companies are in the business of providing fire protection services, including on-call or on-site firefighting teams, to other businesses and institutions.

In addition to career firefighters, there are close to a million volunteer or paid-call firefighters nationwide. These individuals work mostly in rural or small communities and may receive compensation only when they are called to duty, or they may receive no monetary compensation at all but get free training and a uniform allowance.

FAST-GROWING GEOGRAPHIC LOCATIONS

You might consider relocating in your quest for a career firefighter position, because there are greater opportunities in some areas of the country than others. According to the Bureau of Labor Statistics, the states expected to increase their hiring of firefighters in the 10-year period from 1996 to 2006 include Utah, New Mexico, Idaho, and Arizona. Following close behind are Nevada, Florida, New Hampshire, Colorado, Alabama, and Washington state. Those employing the most firefighters and always looking for more include California, with an expected force of 30,750 in the year 2006; Texas, with 18,450; and Illinois, with 13,500. In contrast, there are a few states that expect to reduce their forces by 2006; they include New Jersey, Rhode Island, and Wyoming. When reading Chapter 2, keep in mind that the states whose forces are growing are ones in which you might consider applying for a job.

WOMEN IN THE FIRE PROTECTION FIELD

Although traditionally a male-dominated profession, firefighting has undergone changes in the past 50 years, recognizing that many women can perform the job alongside men. The first known woman firefighter in the United States was an African American woman named Molly Williams. Williams was a slave, owned by a member of Oceanus Engine Company #11 in New York City. She was known to work in a calico dress and checked apron and was said to be "as good a fire laddie as many of the boys." During the blizzard of 1818, Williams distinguished herself by working in harsh conditions when male firefighters were scarce. Over the next hundred years, a handful of women worked as career or volunteer firefighters.

It was during World War II that large numbers of women were given the opportunity to work in fire departments around the country, to take the place of men who were serving in the military. After the war, the trend continued, and in many cities all-women departments, paid and volunteer, were formed. In the beginning of the twenty-first century, there are an estimated 5,000 to 5,200 career women firefighters. They represent less than 3% of the entire force, but their numbers are growing. In addition, there are an estimated 30,000 to 40,000 women volunteers and on-call firefighters. As they gain seniority and experience, women are being promoted in fire departments around the country. The chart below gives recent numbers for each state.

State	Number of Women and Breakdown
Alabama	33 women on 9 departments
	(19 are on the Birmingham FD)
	1 engineer, 2 captains
Alaska	11 women on 3 departments
	2 engineers
Arizona	113 women on 18 departments
	(81 are on the Phoenix and Tucson FDs)
	14 engineers, 3 lieutenants, 12 captains, 1 chief
Arkansas	13 women on 6 departments
	(9 on the Little Rock and North Little Rock FDs)
California	1,008 women on 125 departments
	(570 women are on the CDF, San Francisco, Los Angeles City, and San Diego FDs)
	96 engineers (70 on the CDF), 5 lieutenants, 51 captains, 11 chiefs, 2 department chiefs
Colorado	143 women on 24 departments
	(89 women are on the Colorado Springs, Denver, Aurora, and Boulder FDs)
	4 engineers, 8 lieutenants, 2 captains, 1 chief
Connecticut	55 women on 27 departments
	1 lieutenant
Delaware	6 women on 1 department
District of Columbia	42 women on 1 department
	1 sergeant, 1 lieutenant
Florida	655 women on 110 departments
	(194 are on the Miami-Dade County and Orange County FDs)
	16 engineers, 35 lieutenants, 9 captains, 10 chiefs, 1 department chief
Georgia	77 women on 24 departments
	2 lieutenants, 1 captain, 3 chiefs, 1 department chief
Guam	1 woman on 1 department
Hawaii	9 women on 4 departments
	1 captain
Idaho	2 women on 2 departments

State	Number of Women and Breakdown
Illinois	173 women on 58 departments
	(80 are on the Chicago FD)
	2 engineers, 6 lieutenants, 1 captain, 1 department chief
Indiana	72 women on 23 departments
	2 engineers, 3 lieutenants, 2 captains, 4 chiefs, 1 department chief
Iowa	35 women on 12 departments
Kansas	29 women on 12 departments
	(12 are on the Topeka FD)
	2 engineers, 3 lieutenants, 1 captain
Kentucky	26 women on 10 departments
	1 engineer, 1 lieutenant, 2 captains, 1 chief
Louisiana	74 women on 11 departments
	(61 are on the Shreveport and Baton Rouge FDs)
	1 engineer, 1 lieutenant, 2 captains
Maine	6 women on 6 departments
	1 lieutenant
Maryland	224 women on 7 departments
	(100 are on the Montgomery County FD)
	1 sergeant, 4 lieutenants, 3 captains, 4 chiefs
Massachusetts	65 women on 44 departments
	4 lieutenants, 1 captain
Michigan	135 women on 23 departments
	2 engineers, 9 lieutenants, 2 captains, 1 chief
Minnesota	57 women on 6 departments
	(38 are on the Minneapolis FD)
	1 engineer, 9 captains, 1 chief
Mississippi	24 women on 9 departments
	(10 are on the Jackson FD)
	1 engineer, 1 lieutenant, 2 captains
Missouri	64 women on 26 departments
	2 engineers, 7 captains, 1 chief
Montana	No women known to be career firefighters for structural fire agencies

State	Number of Women and Breakdown
Nebraska	21 women on 4 departments
	(17 are on the Omaha FD)
	2 captains
Nevada	63 women on 6 departments
	3 engineers, 6 captains
New Hampshire	13 women on 10 departments
	1 chief
New Jersey	8 women on 6 departments
	1 lieutenant
New Mexico	34 women on 9 departments
	(23 are on the Albuquerque and Bernalillo County FDs)
	1 engineer, 1 lieutenant, 1 chief
New York	71 women on 18 departments
	(36 are on the New York City FD)
	2 fire marshals, 3 lieutenants, 1 captain
North Carolina	129 women on 30 departments
	5 engineers, 6 lieutenants, 10 captains, 3 chiefs, 1 department chief
North Dakota	4 women on 3 departments
Ohio	180 women on 54 departments
	9 lieutenants, 7 captains, 2 chiefs
Oklahoma	27 women on 7 departments
	(17 are on the Oklahoma City FD)
	4 captains, 1 chief
Oregon	64 women on 16 departments
	2 engineers, 4 lieutenants, 2 chiefs
Pennsylvania	43 women on 11 departments
	(21 are on the Pittsburgh FD)
	2 lieutenants, 1 captain
Puerto Rico	1 woman on 1 department
	1 lieutenant
Rhode Island	13 women on 8 departments
	(6 are on the Providence FD)
South Carolina	14 women on 10 departments
	1 captain

State	Number of Women and Breakdown
South Dakota	4 women on 2 departments
Tennessee	66 women on 16 departments
	9 engineers, 4 lieutenants
Texas	306 women on 45 departments
	(139 are on the Houston and Dallas FDs)
	17 engineers, 9 lieutenants, 3 captains, 2 chiefs
Utah	17 women on 8 departments
	1 captain, 1 chief
Vermont	5 women on 3 departments
Virginia	206 women on 25 departments
	1 engineer, 7 lieutenants, 3 captains, 1 chief, 2 department chiefs
Washington	199 women on 26 departments
	(120 are on the Seattle and Tacoma FDs)
	1 engineer, 11 lieutenants, 3 captains, 5 chiefs, 1 department chief
West Virginia	15 women on 4 departments
Wisconsin	121 women on 25 departments
	(76 are on the Madison and Milwaukee FDs)
	2 engineers, 11 lieutenants, 1 captain, 2 chiefs, 1 department chief
Wyoming	1 woman on 1 department
	1 company officer

Source: Women in the Fire Service, Inc. Copyright © 1999 Women in the Fire Service, Inc. Reprinted with permission

JOB OPPORTUNITIES IN THE FIRE PROTECTION FIELD

Many people are needed to fight fires, both on the front lines and behind the scenes. While the majority of firefighters work for municipal fire departments, there are also jobs available in the private sector, the military, and state and federal governments. Several opportunities exist for volunteer firefighters in many locations across the country. In addition to these frontline positions, which deal mainly with actual fire suppression, there are other, less visible jobs in the fire-fighting field. These positions focus on fire prevention, and include fire protection engineers and fire inspectors. They make sure buildings and other sites are following safety codes; they can spot and correct fire hazards before a fire has a chance to start.

Listed below is more specific information on many of the entry-level job opportunities in the firefighting field. Keep in mind that job descriptions, minimum requirements, and typical salaries vary from position to position. As you consider your future career, you will need this information to help you decide which type of firefighting job best suits you.

IN THE NEWS

Careless smoking accounts for no less than a third of fire deaths in New York, prompting the governor to pass a bill in June of 2000 requiring fire-safe cigarettes. Tobacco companies will have to develop and sell cigarettes that extinguish themselves when they are not being actively smoked.

Fire Suppression

As stated above, the most visible jobs in the firefighting field involve fire suppression. These are the men and women who work to actively put out existing fires and offer assistance in emergency situations such as car accidents, terrorist activities, and hazardous material spills.

Municipal Firefighter

Nine out of 10 firefighters work for municipal (local government) fire departments. Since this is the most common job in the firefighting field, it's the one about which you've probably heard the most. These are the firefighters who are paid, full-time workers (also called career firefighters, to distinguish them from volunteer or part-time firefighters). They fight fires and respond to emergency situations within their local community and may be called by surrounding fire departments to offer mutual aid for extremely serious fires.

Municipal firefighters work in teams and are assigned specific tasks to ensure optimal organization at the scene of a fire. Most fire departments have a combination of one or more of the following: engine company, ladder company, pump company, and truck company. Firefighters are assigned to one of these companies within the fire department, so they know exactly what they need to focus on when a fire call comes in. Some firefighters become apparatus operators (also known as fire truck drivers) after serving as firefighters for some time and passing a promotional exam; some are assigned pump duty; some enter burning structures to search for survivors; some handle the ladders while other firefighters are busy axing their way through the roof. Every fire call is different, but firefighters work together in an organized and systematic way by following the orders of their leader. He or she may be the fire chief, the assistant fire chief, the captain, or a person with some other title, depending on the size and location of the fire department.

There are several levels of rank for firefighters in municipal departments and many opportunities for promotion and advancement, depending on the size and location of the department. Most fire departments have a combination of the following job titles and ranks:

Firefighter Recruit	Battalion Chief
Firefighter Level I	District Chief
Firefighter Level II	Deputy Chief
Apparatus Operator (Truck Driver)	Assistant Fire Chief
Fire Lieutenant	Fire Chief
Fire Captain	

After completing the application process for a municipal firefighting position, applicants are rated and either placed on an eligibility list or eliminated from the process. If you are called from this list and you pass all subsequent tests and interviews and are hired, you move on to a training program. You'll be called a probationary firefighter (known as a "probie" to insiders) for the first 6 to 18 months, depending on the length of probation required in your area. See Chapter 5 for information about advancement opportunities within municipal fire departments.

Typical Minimum Requirements

While requirements vary, most municipal fire departments require applicants to have a high school diploma or GED, be at least 18 years old, and pass a physical ability exam. Some states require that state certification be obtained by prospective firefighters before they are considered for a job. Since there is such intense competition for job openings, however, many applicants go well above the minimum requirements by getting volunteer firefighting experience and specialized training from a college fire science program to gain an edge on the competition.

Education beyond high school in other fields of study can also improve your chances of landing a job, as more and more departments are asking that candidates have some college credit. Chapter 3 has specific information about education, including fire science training programs. Other requirements may include no smoking, drug use (you will be tested during the application process), and U.S. citizenship.

Typical Salaries

While income varies greatly depending on the location and availability of funds in each fire department, most firefighters earn a good salary, especially as they advance and attain higher levels of training. See the table below for firefighter salaries in a number of locations to get an idea of what you can expect (figures are from the Labor Relations Information System; for the most recently compiled numbers, check out its website at www.lris.com/index.html). As stated earlier, you might want to consider relocating to an area of the country where firefighters are paid better if you find that your state comes in on the low end of the pay scale. You can also find recent salary information in the annual publication entitled *Municipal Year Book*, found in the reference department of your local public library.

Location	Annual Salary
San Jose, California	$57,888
Anchorage, Alaska	$56,304
Jersey City, New Jersey	$55,824
Schaumburg, Illinois	$53,928
Pensacola, Florida	$29,100
Louisville, Kentucky	$27,864
Pontiac, Michigan	$20,940
Monroe, Louisiana	$15,360

Volunteer and Paid-Call Firefighter

It is estimated that of the over one million firefighters in the United States, 815,500 are volunteers. Many prospective career firefighters become volunteer firefighters first, so they can gain experience. Volunteering also allows them to use their skills as they conduct their job search or wait for their number to be called from eligibility lists of paid departments. There is often a large time commitment required by many volunteer fire departments, and their firefighters receive little or no monetary compensation for their work. Volunteers are those who work for no pay, while paid-call firefighters usually receive minimum wage or a similar level of earnings for each fire call that they go on.

Volunteers may serve with career firefighters in the same fire company or they may comprise an entire fire company, with only a paid fire chief and assistant who work full-time for the department. Some volunteer firefighters are given pagers, so they don't have to spend much time in the fire station waiting for calls. If they are on call and their pager goes off, they put a blue light/siren in the window of their car and drive to the fire station. There they get on the fire truck and head to the fire. Volunteer firefighters who are properly certified can perform the same functions that paid career firefighters do.

The experience you receive as a volunteer firefighter can be different, depending on the type of crew you work with. If you become a volunteer who works with a full crew of paid career firefighters, you can get an inside look at how things are run in the firehouse and at fires by a municipal department. This type of volunteer spends a specified number of hours at the firehouse instead of getting a pager and going on-call. However, there may be some adjustment needed to fit in with the career firefighters when you are the only volunteer on duty. Some volunteers prefer a firefighting crew that is made up of all volunteers, to give them a feeling of camaraderie.

Typical Minimum Requirements

Requirements for volunteers have grown over the past 25 years. Although some counties and states still ask only that volunteers sign up and pass a physical exam, most demand extensive training. The typical training requirement includes a 100–150-hour course, plus another 75–100 hours of training if the department provides emergency medical care. Many volunteers are also given annual hazardous materials training, which ranges from 10–25 hours. In addition, they may be required to recertify their training every three to five years.

Jeffrey Cuttitta, a volunteer firefighter in Long Island, New York, said he went through several procedures before being selected to serve: a physical exam, 10 weeks of classroom and 10 weeks of hands-on training, a wait for an opening, and a swearing in. After joining the department, he became a "probie." He then had to pass a written and a physical exam, attend all meetings and drills, and go to a predetermined number of fire calls for one year to get off of probationary status. Once the probationary period ended, Cuttitta went on to attain Firefighter I certification from the local fire academy.

Typical Salaries

While volunteers usually don't get paid, they enjoy several benefits: gaining firefighting experience, getting to know career firefighters, and learning to work as a team. Some volunteers do get small allowances to pay for their transportation to and from the fire department, and paid-call firefighters usually get minimum wage or a similar level of pay for each hour they spend on a fire call.

State Wildland Firefighter

Many state government agencies hire firefighters to protect state-owned land. Every year, these agencies have to deal with the threat of wildfires—fast-spreading burns that can scorch thousands of acres. These wildfires are often in remote regions with limited access, which makes fighting them perilous and brutal work. Fires on this scale are controlled not by using fire hoses, but by limiting where and how much the fire burns.

The states that employ the most firefighters are located in the western portion of the United States, since these states have the most forests or wildlands. However, other states employ limited numbers of state firefighters too. For example, in Minnesota, the Department of Natural Resources (DNR) has two divisions that hire seasonal firefighters: the forestry division and the state park division.

Most entry-level state firefighters are hired only during the season when most fires occur—and the fire season varies in each area of the country. Arizona, for instance, often employs firefighters from March to July (when monsoons arrive and fires are put out naturally) and then again in October if it is a dry year. California often doesn't hire until May, but its season can last until December.

Seasonal wildland fire fighting differs from structural firefighting because of the nature and location of the fire. Much of the work is hard manual labor, such as cutting down brush and trees that are in the way of the fire. Excellent physical condition is required to keep up the pace of hard work for several days in a row as the fire rages. Most wildland fires last much longer than structural fires.

The California Department of Forestry calls itself the largest fire department in the country (at the state level), because it employs from 2,500 to 3,500 firefighters every fire season. The state posts its openings for firefighters each year, and in 1996 more than 10,000 applications were received, meaning that there is great competition for these jobs. The filing deadline is usually in January or early February, and if you miss it, you must wait until the following year to sign up. Many states, though, such as those in the southeast, often find themselves running short of personnel, particularly during the peak of the fire season.

Typical Minimum Requirements

Excellent physical condition is required for wildland firefighters due to the heavy manual labor, harsh conditions, longevity, and intensity of wildland fires. A good work record will increase your chances of getting hired, even if it is in an unrelated field. Because of the outdoor nature of the work, it is also advisable that applicants possess such skills as the ability to pitch a tent, cook over an open fire, and sharpen a knife. Knowledge of basic first aid and CPR (cardiopulmonary resuscitation) can also improve a candidate's chances of getting hired, as can proficiency with chain saws and trucks with 5-and-a-2 transmission. Every state requires that you be at least 18 years old and possess a high school diploma or its equivalent. There are additional requirements that vary from state to state, including having U.S. citizenship, not abusing alcohol or drugs, and passing a civil service exam.

Typical Salaries

The salaries are normally lower for entry-level state firefighters than they are for entry-level municipal firefighters, and the work is seasonal rather than year-round. The pay ranges from $8.30 to $10.00 per hour, but many firefighters get significantly more by adding overtime and hazard (actual frontline fighting) pay to their base pay. Also, firefighters who live in communities that have a high cost of living may receive higher wages.

Federal Wildland Firefighter

As with the state-level job described above, federal wildland firefighters fight fires in forests or wildlands. However, they are hired by the U.S. Department of the Interior and the U.S. Department of Agriculture and charged with protecting federal lands and parks rather than those maintained by individual states. The blazes these firefighters fight are caused both by human and natural forces, including, for example, the campfire that gets out of control and the bolt of lightning that hits dry brush. Similar to their state-level counterparts, federal firefighters also must engage in hard physical labor to stop raging forest or wildland fires.

For example, crews may be rushed into an area that is threatened and told to "scrape it down to mineral." This means that all the vegetation—dried grass, plants, dead wood, and anything else that would burn—has to be removed. This method of fire fighting stops a fire by cutting back its fuel. In the wilds, this work may involve a four-person crew scraping an eight-foot-wide path for two miles. They must work fast, in hot, dry conditions, as the front of the fire approaches. Other tactics include starting and controlling a small fire and guiding it toward the front of the original fire to take away its fuel.

Large, raging wildland or forest fires can be like wars. Firefighting crews are flown and trucked in; air tankers are coordinated with the ground troops; support crews providing food, medical and mail services converge on the scene. The shifts for firefighters can run 16–24 hours or more of hard physical labor in heavy gear as the air temperature often exceeds 100 degrees, which is why you need to be in excellent physical shape.

There are various levels and duties for federal firefighters. The first step is usually to work for a national forest, becoming a general wildland firefighter (referred to as a type-two firefighter) who works to support the frontline fire fighting crew (called type-one firefighters). The next move up would be to join an engine company, work up to a type-one crew, the members of which are called hot shots and fight at the front line of the fire. Finally, you can apply to become a smoke jumper. Currently there are approximately 2,200 firefighters who work as part of a hot-shot type-one team and about 360 smoke jumpers nationwide, with several thousand type-two firefighters. Timo Rivo, a smoke jumper who works out of Montana, explains the exciting role of a smoke jumper:

> Smoke jumpers parachute out of airplanes to fight fires where no ground access is available. We carry heavy packs of supplies and stay out on the fire for up to three days before new provisions are dropped in to us or we leave the area. Sometimes we end up walking out after we conquer the fire and it might be a 16-mile trek back to the ground crew headquarters. Other times, we get a lift out on a helicopter, but overall, it is very demanding work. We need to pass grueling physical tests every year to maintain smoke jumper status.

Many federal firefighters are flown to different states to fight fires in a variety of locations throughout the fire season, depending on need and weather patterns. The agencies of the federal government that hire the most firefighters are the National Park Service, the Bureau of Land Management (both in the Department of the Interior) and the Forest Service (in the Department of Agriculture). See Appendix A for information on how to contact them.

Typical Minimum Requirements

Standards vary among the different branches of the federal government, but in general, applicants need to pass a physical agility test, be at least 18 years old, and have a high school diploma or its equivalent. The government ranks all of its jobs by grade, which also determines salary. The grade of the position(s) available is always included on a job listing and must be repeated on an application. There is more detailed information on finding and applying for federal jobs in the Chapter 2.

For an entry-level position, at least three months of "general work experience" are also necessary. The government defines this as "any type of work that demonstrates your ability to perform the work of the position." For a position above entry-level, work experience and education requirements increase. For a job at grade GS-5, you would need a year of specialized work experience (directly related to the job you are applying for), and a bachelor's degree with courses taken in a related field.

Typical Salaries

The salary for an entry-level federal firefighter (grade GS-2) starts at $7.98 per hour, but many firefighters get significantly more by adding overtime and hazard pay to their base. A move up to a position at grade GS-6 can entitle you to earn $12.19 per hour. A federal firefighter from Minnesota with over five years of experience earned $12.00 an hour in 1997. However, during some years he was able to make as much as $26,000 in one fire season due to extensive overtime and hazard pay. The salaries for seasonal federal firefighters can vary greatly, depending on the length and severity of the fire season.

Military Firefighter

Another federal employer of firefighters is the U.S. Department of Defense. There is a range of opportunities in the different branches of the military for various types of firefighting. Most, however, involve the protection of military bases. Military bases employ enlisted men and women (and some civilians) to become base firefighters instead of relying on the local municipal fire department. Since the job duties of a military firefighter are similar to those of a municipal firefighter's, the job offers good experience to someone who wants to apply for a municipal firefighting job upon completion of military service.

Approximately 2,200 firefighters are employed by the military, and approximately 350 new firefighters are needed each year. While all branches of the military employ firefighters, the two branches of the military that train and employ the most firefighters are the Air Force and the Navy. The Air Force trains firefighters in how to protect aircraft when accidents occur during takeoffs and landings as well as how to fight structural fires and deal with hazardous materials. A 13-week fire academy training course, covering the basics of fire-fighting, is offered at the Goodfellow Air Force Base in San Angelo, Texas. The Air Force gives firefighters training on a regular basis, and their training courses offer students college credit from the Community College of the Air Force. Therefore many Air Force firefighters can obtain an associate's degree through this ongoing training.

Most Air Force bases employ a mix of military members and civilians. Since military members are often moved around to different bases, depending on need, the civilian firefighters remain at the same base to maintain a sense of continuity. According to Floyd Virgil, a military firefighter at the Keesler Air Force Base, several of the civilian firefighters who work at the base were previous military firefighters retired from active duty, so they came with experience when they applied for the job. He also states that military firefighters have a good chance of getting hired outside the military because it is well known that the military has excellent fire service training programs.

If this position interests you and you are not already enlisted in the Air Force, your first step is to contact a recruiter (listed in the yellow pages of your local phone book). In your initial meeting, ask the recruiter if you can get a guarantee of being trained and placed in the fire protection field. If you achieve a high enough score on the skills tests (the Armed Services Vocational Aptitude Battery, or ASVAB) and pass all other requirements, the Air Force may guarantee in writing that your career area will be within the fire protection field as a part of your enlistment agreement.

After you enlist, you will undergo six weeks of basic training at Lackland Air Force Base in San Antonio, Texas. If you have fire protection guaranteed as your career area, you will then be sent to the Goodfellow Air Force Base in San Angelo, Texas, for the 13-week training program before being assigned to a fire department. Air Force enlistment periods are for three to six years.

The Navy's firefighters are trained to combat fires on its fleet of ships as well as other, related operations. This type of firefighting is often called damage control within the Navy. You can also check into getting a job with the aircraft fire rescue team in the Navy for aircraft that crash into the water. The Navy offers certified apprenticeship programs for some specialties within the firefighting occupation.

The increased visibility of firefighting in the Navy is evidenced by the establishment of a new award in 1994, the Homer W. Carhart Award for Fire Protection Excellence. Dr. Homer W. Carhart is a Senior Scientist Emeritus at the Naval Research Laboratory (NRL) in Washington, DC. He is an expert in the areas of safety, fire protection, and shipboard survivability, with over 50 years of experience in these areas. The award was established by the Chief of Naval Operations to recognize superior achievement in the areas of safety and shipboard survivability.

As with the Air Force, if you are not already enlisted, you must first contact a recruiter. This person will begin your application process by screening for minimum requirements and disqualifications. If the Navy accepts you, you will be sent for eight weeks and three days of basic training in Great Lakes, Illinois. You can choose to enlist in the Navy for a period of three, four, five, or six years.

Typical Minimum Requirements

The minimum requirements for all branches of the military are nearly identical. They require that their recruits

- ▶ be between 17 and 29 years of age
- ▶ be a U. S. citizens or have legal immigrant alien status
- ▶ have a clean arrest record
- ▶ be in good health and excellent physical condition
- ▶ pass a medical exam, including drug testing

To become a firefighter in the military, you also need to achieve an acceptable score on the ASVAB prior to enlisting. At this printing, applicants need to achieve a score of 39 in the general category to be admitted to the fire protection career area.

Typical Salaries

Salaries for firefighters in the military are calculated in the same way as those for other military jobs. They may be found on the military base pay chart, found on page 24, which takes rank and years of service into account. The dollar amounts in the table combine basic pay, basic allowance for quarters, basic allowance for subsistence, and the average variable housing allowance. They also include the tax advantage from untaxed allowances. The figures do not include the average overseas housing allowance or the overseas cost-of-living allowance.

The 2000 Military Pay Chart

Grade	<2	2	3	4	6	8	10	12	14	16	18	20	22	24
Commissioned Officers														
0-10	8214.90	8503.80	8503.80	8503.80	8503.80	8830.20	8830.20	9319.50	9319.50	9986.40	9986.40	10655.10	10655.10	10655.10
0-9	7280.70	7471.50	7630.50	7630.50	7630.50	7824.60	7824.60	8150.10	8150.10	8830.20	8830.20	9319.50	9319.50	9319.50
0-8	6594.30	6792.30	6953.10	6953.10	6953.10	7471.50	7471.50	7824.60	7824.60	8150.10	8503.80	8830.20	9048.00	9048.00
0-7	5479.50	5851.80	5851.80	5851.80	6114.60	6114.60	6468.90	6468.90	6792.30	7471.50	7985.40	7985.40	7985.40	7985.40
0-6	4061.10	4461.60	4754.40	4754.40	4754.40	4754.40	4754.40	4754.40	4916.10	5693.10	5983.80	6114.60	6468.90	6687.30
0-5	3248.40	3813.90	4077.90	4077.90	4077.90	4077.90	4200.30	4427.10	4723.80	5077.50	5368.30	5531.10	5724.60	5724.60
0-4	2737.80	3333.90	3556.20	3556.20	3622.20	3781.80	4040.40	4267.50	4461.60	4658.10	4785.90	4785.90	4785.90	4785.90
0-3	2544.00	2844.30	3041.10	3364.80	3525.90	3652.20	3850.20	4040.40	4139.10	4139.10	4139.10	4139.10	4139.10	4139.10
0-2	2218.80	2423.10	2910.90	3009.00	3071.10	3071.10	3071.10	3071.10	3071.10	3071.10	3071.10	3071.10	3071.10	3071.10
0-1	1926.30	2004.90	2423.10	2423.10	2423.10	2423.10	2423.10	2423.10	2423.10	2423.10	2423.10	2423.10	2423.10	2423.10
Commissioned Officers with over 4 years active duty service as an enlisted member or warrant officer														
0-3E	0.00	0.00	0.00	3364.80	3525.90	3652.20	3850.20	4040.40	4200.30	4200.30	4200.30	4200.30	4200.30	4200.30
0-2E	0.00	0.00	0.00	3009.00	3071.10	3168.60	3333.90	3461.40	3556.20	3556.20	3556.20	3556.20	3556.20	3556.20
0-1E	0.00	0.00	0.00	2423.10	2588.40	2683.80	2781.30	2877.60	3009.00	3009.00	3009.00	3009.00	3009.00	3009.00
Warrant Officers														
W-5	0.00	0.00	0.00	0.00	0.00	0.00	0.00	0.00	0.00	0.00	0.00	4423.80	4591.20	4724.10
W-4	2592.00	2781.30	2781.30	2844.30	2974.20	3105.00	3235.50	3461.40	3622.20	3749.40	3850.20	3874.10	4107.00	4235.10
W-3	2355.90	2555.40	2555.40	2588.40	2618.70	2810.40	2974.20	3071.10	3168.60	3263.40	3364.80	3495.90	3622.20	3622.20
W-2	2063.40	2232.60	2232.60	2297.40	2423.10	2555.40	2652.60	2749.80	2844.30	2944.50	3041.10	3136.80	3263.40	3263.40
W-1	1719.00	1971.00	1971.00	2135.90	2232.60	2328.00	2423.10	2522.70	2618.70	2716.20	2810.40	2910.90	2910.90	2910.90

The 2000 Military Pay Chart (Continued)

Grade	\<2	2	3	4	6	8	10	12	14	16	18	20	22	24
							Years of Service							
Enlisted Members														
E-9	0.00	0.00	0.00	0.00	0.00	0.00	3015.30	3083.40	3152.70	3225.60	3298.20	3361.50	3537.90	3675.60
E-8	0.00	0.00	0.00	0.00	0.00	2528.40	2601.60	2669.70	2739.00	2811.60	2875.50	2946.30	3119.40	3258.00
E-7	1765.80	1906.20	1976.10	2045.70	2115.60	2182.80	2252.70	2323.20	2427.90	2496.90	2566.20	2599.50	2774.40	2912.40
E-6	1518.90	1655.70	1724.40	1797.50	1865.40	1932.60	2003.40	2106.60	2172.90	2242.80	2277.00	2277.00	2277.00	2277.00
E-5	1332.60	1450.50	1521.00	1587.30	1691.70	1761.00	1830.00	1898.10	1932.60	1932.60	1932.60	1932.60	1932.60	1932.60
E-4	1242.90	1312.80	1390.20	1497.30	1556.70	1556.70	1556.70	1556.70	1556.70	1556.70	1556.70	1556.70	1556.70	1556.70
E-3	1171.50	1235.70	1284.60	1335.90	1335.90	1335.90	1335.90	1335.90	1335.90	1335.90	1335.90	1335.90	1335.90	1335.90
E-2	1127.40	1127.40	1127.40	1127.40	1127.40	1127.40	1127.40	1127.40	1127.40	1127.40	1127.40	1127.40	1127.40	1127.40
E-1\>4	1005.60	1005.60	1005.60	1005.60	1005.60	1005.60	1005.60	1005.60	1005.60	1005.60	1005.60	1005.60	1005.60	1005.60
E-1\<4	930.30	0.00	0.00	0.00	0.00	0.00	0.00	0.00	0.00	0.00	0.00	0.00	0.00	0.00

Key to Military Ranks

Army Ranks:

E-1: Recruit
E-2: Private
E-3: Private First Class
E-4: Corporal/Specialist
E-5: Sergeant
E-6: Staff Sergeant
E-7: Sergeant First Class
E-8: Master Sergeant
E-9: Sergeant Major

Navy Ranks:

E-1: Airman or Seaman or Fireman or Construction Recruit
E-2: Airman or Seaman or Fireman or Construction Apprentice
E-3: Airman or Seaman or Fireman or Construction
E-4: Petty Officer 3rd Class
E-5: Petty Officer 2nd Class
E-6: Petty Officer 1st Class
E-7: Chief Petty Officer
E-8: Senior Chief Petty Officer
E-9: Master Chief Petty Officer

Air Force Ranks:

E-1: Airman basic
E-2: Airman
E-3: Airman 1st Class
E-4: Senior Airman
E-5: Staff Sergeant
E-6: Technical Sergeant
E-7: Master Sergeant
E-8: Senior Master Sergeant
E-9: Chief Master Sergeant

Marine Ranks:

E-1: Private
E-2: Private First Class
E-3: Lance Corporal
E-4: Corporal
E-5: Sergeant
E-6: Staff Sergeant
E-7: Gunnery Sergeant
E-8: Either Master Sergeant or 1st Sergeant
E-9: Master Gunnery Sergeant or Sergeant Major

Coast Guard Ranks:

E-1: Recruit
E-2: Fireman or Seaman Apprentice
E-3: Fireman or Seaman
E-4: Petty Officer 3rd Class
E-5: Petty Officer 2nd Class
E-6: Petty Officer 1st Class
E-7: Chief Petty Officer
E-8: Senior Chief Petty Officer

Firefighters in Private Companies

In addition to the many job opportunities offered by government agencies, there are firefighting jobs available with private companies. You can look for jobs from the following types of businesses:

▶ oil and chemical refineries
▶ large corporations

▶ airports

▶ shipyards

A majority of private-sector jobs for firefighters can be found with companies in the petrochemical, aircraft, and aerospace industries such as Boeing. Many private firefighters become highly specialized by focusing their training and inspection activities to one location and the major threat in that area, such as oil fires at an oil company or airplane fires in an airport.

There is a growing trend for private firefighting companies to set up shop to provide firefighters to various companies, sometimes along with additional fire prevention and protection services. One such company is Rural/Metro Corporation, which currently provides fire protection services to more than 25 communities and responds to more than 60,000 calls annually. It is based in Arizona but has offices across the nation. You may find job opportunities with private companies by searching the Internet with a search engine such as Yahoo.com or Google.com. Try using search terms such as "firefighting" and "employment" or "fire suppression" and "jobs."

Typical Minimum Requirements
The minimum requirements for each private company vary. In general, as with most firefighting positions, applicants should be in good physical condition and have solid work experience to get the best opportunities for firefighting jobs in the private sector. Some specialized training, such as having hazardous materials certification when applying to oil and chemical companies, could also prove beneficial. Many private firefighting companies have a selection process similar to that of municipal fire departments, and require thorough written and physical testing and some form of fire service training before hiring applicants.

Typical Salaries
Salaries vary among the different private fire companies, just as they do in other private industries. However, most companies will have salaries similar to that of municipal firefighting departments, in order to recruit high-quality applicants.

EMT Firefighter

Firefighter EMTs or paramedics are trained to provide emergency medical care, including ambulance services. They respond to a variety of emergency situations as well as fires. For example, they assist victims of natural disasters and spills of hazardous materials as well as medical emergencies, such as heart attacks, strokes, and choking. They assess, manage, and administer treatment to ill or injured persons on the way to hospitals or other medical facilities, most often in a life-support unit or an ambulance. EMTs rely on radio communication to transmit information about a patient's condition and to receive medical instruction from a physician or other medical professional. The level of treatment they are allowed to provide depends upon their level of training and certification.

Three levels of EMT certification are recognized by the National Registry of Emergency Medical Technicians: Basic, Intermediate, and Paramedic. Training programs are offered nationwide from colleges and universities; hospitals; and police, fire, and government health departments. Most EMT-Basic programs are modeled on a 110-hour standard training course developed by the U.S. Department of Transportation. Candidates must meet certain minimum requirements (for example, a minimum age of 18, high school diploma or GED, and valid driver's license). Programs for EMT-Intermediate and EMT-Paramedic cover progressively more advanced levels of medical treatment and require completion of the prior level(s) of training.

Some fire departments, such as Atlanta, Georgia's, now require all new firefighter recruits to become certified as an EMT-Basic or EMT-Paramedic on a routine basis instead of allowing firefighters to choose to specialize in this area. Large urban departments in particular look for or require EMT training, due to their high level of responsibility for providing emergency medical services in the community.

Typical Minimum Requirements

To acquire EMT-Basic certification, you need to complete an approved training program, usually consisting of approximately 100 to 120 hours of study. EMT-Intermediate certification requires approximately 35 to 55 hours of instruction in addition to EMT-Basic training. EMT-Paramedic is the most advanced level of EMT training and requires approximately

750–2,000 hours of training in total (including the EMT-Basic and EMT-Intermediate hours of training). EMT-Paramedics often complete an associate in science degree in the course of their training.

Typical Salaries

EMT firefighters earn salaries above those of firefighters without EMT training. Base annual salaries for EMT firefighters in cities around the country are as follows:

Boston, Massachusetts	$36,452
Fort Worth, Texas	$34,992
Washington, DC	$32,436
Chicago, Illinois	$32,000
Miami, Florida	$31,654
Houston, Texas	$29,925
Phoenix, Arizona	$29,224
Charlotte, North Carolina	$23,778 (includes incentive pay for education)

Fire Prevention

We have covered the most popular positions in the area of fire suppression, which involves the act of physically fighting fires. But the firefighting field is also made up of those who work to prevent fires. Fire inspectors and fire prevention engineers help to protect the public by making our structures and vehicles safer before and after they are built and by educating us about fire safety and fire prevention.

Fire Inspector

Most fire inspectors' work involves commercial or other nonresidential structures. They examine these buildings to eliminate fire hazards and to monitor fire protection equipment, such as sprinkler systems, extinguishers, and alarms, to ensure operability. Inspectors also patrol industrial sites to determine if hazardous and combustible materials are stored properly. According to Kevin Scarbrough, an experienced fire inspector in Ann Arbor, Michigan, many inspectors focus on the construction of new buildings to ensure that they meet all required state and local fire codes as they are being built. Some also offer fire education information to schools and local civic groups.

The job of fire inspector is held both by those trained in fire inspection procedures and by experienced firefighters who took promotions and gained additional training to land the position, depending on the organizational structure and size of the fire department. Historically, the fire inspector was a firefighter first and then learned the duties of fire inspection through promotional exams. The growing trend now is for fire departments or fire prevention bureaus to hire entry-level fire inspectors who have specialized college-level training but no firefighting experience.

Typical Minimum Requirements

Depending on the fire agency doing the hiring, requirements vary greatly. You must have a high school diploma and at least four years of experience in the field. In some fire departments, you have to serve as a firefighter for several years (anywhere from 4 to 15 years or more) to be eligible for promotion to inspector. Other fire departments open up the position of fire inspector to graduates of fire science degree programs who have never served as firefighters. Skills that most departments look for are the abilities to lead the work of others, perform many complicated tasks, and plan and accomplish goals.

Typical Salaries

Salaries vary among departments and locations, but the median ranges from $48,778 to $59,099. Those figures include salaries for both entry-level fire inspectors and long-term firefighters promoted to inspector. For those who have been firefighters for several years before being promoted, the salary range is high relative to that for entry-level fire inspectors. The highest salary awarded in the nation is in Philadelphia, where fire inspectors earn $72,513.

Fire Protection Engineer

This is a field in which the hiring demand is at a high point and should stay there for a number of years. In fact, the need for qualified fire protection engineers is so high that many companies actively recruit on college campuses where fire engineers receive their training. Fire protection engineers take advanced courses in mathematics, physics, and chemistry to gain scientific knowledge used in the research, design, installation, and operation of physical systems related to fire safety. They often work outside of fire departments, usually in the private sector. The majority of fire protection engineers do not begin their careers as firefighters.

Fire protection engineers can be called upon to provide a broad range of services. Some perform fire safety evaluations of building and industrial complexes to determine the risks of fire loss and to find the best ways to prevent fires. Others design systems that automatically detect and suppress fires and explosions as well as fire alarm, smoke control, emergency lighting, communication, and exit systems. Fire protection engineers perform research on materials and consumer products or on computer modeling of fire and smoke behavior. Some investigate fires or explosions and prepare technical reports or provide expert courtroom testimony in civil litigation cases.

Many fire protection engineers are hired to oversee the design and operation of safety procedures for large companies. This is an area of major concern to complex manufacturing facilities, such as refineries, chemical plants, and multinational business networks. These companies know that a million dollars spent on prevention and preparation can save tens of millions in cleanup costs and fines, not to mention the invaluable savings in terms of presenting a good image to the public.

Fire protection engineers also work for insurance companies, surveying major facilities and performing research, testing, and analysis. As the computer and electronics industry grows, its special fire prevention needs expand as well. When a room full of high-tech gear is threatened by fire, the best course of action usually is not to turn on water sprinklers. Finding new ways to prevent and suppress fires and save costly equipment is proving to be a viable new avenue for employment.

Architectural and engineering firms, automatic sprinkler companies, large hotel chains, and specialty consulting groups also hire fire protection engineers. Aside from in private-sector companies, they can be found at all levels of government around the world. Other interesting careers in the field include those in trade associations, in testing laboratories, and at colleges and universities.

Typical Minimum Requirements

Fire protection engineers need a more advanced educational background than firefighters do. Their training typically includes a bachelor of science (BS) degree in a traditional engineering field or in fire science and often a master's degree (MA) in fire protection. If you are in high school and considering this career, consult Chapter 3 for information on the colleges and universities that offer the program you need. Start preparing early by taking and doing well in math and science classes.

Typical Salaries

Due to great demand and the high education level they obtain, fire protection engineers normally make more money than career firefighters. Their salaries are competitive in the industry and generally are higher than the average salary for the overall engineering profession, which ranges from $39,000 to $50,000. Below are listed median base salaries in the year 2000 for fire protection engineers in a number of cities around the country.

San Francisco, California	$47,193
New York, New York	$46,708
Orlando, Florida	$45,552
Detroit, Michigan	$44,402
Boston, Massachusetts	$43,998
Philadelphia, Pennsylvania	$42,825
Las Vegas, Nevada	$42,623
Houston, Texas	$42,057
Nashville, Tennessee	$38,215
Jacksonville, Florida	$37,892

IS FIREFIGHTING THE RIGHT CAREER FOR YOU?

You have read the job descriptions listed above for a variety of fire-related positions, and perhaps more than one are appealing to you. To find out which position might best suit you, take the following test. It is designed to help you determine if a career in firefighting or fire prevention is right for you, allowing you to see the traits that fit each field best. Write down your yes or no answers to the following questions and then take a look at what those answers mean by consulting the explanation at the end of the test.

1. Are you physically fit and do you have good upper body strength?
2. Do you enjoy working out and staying in shape?
3. Do you enjoy working in teams?
4. Do you like to get adrenaline rushes?
5. Do you prefer a flexible work schedule?
6. Do you enjoy enforcing rules?
7. Do you like to teach others?
8. Do you smoke cigarettes or cigars?
9. Do you enjoy a daily routine that is similar every day?
10. Do you value a high level of privacy and space at work?
11. Can you follow instructions properly and quickly?
12. Do you enjoy working outdoors?
13. Are you interested in learning about medical emergency technology?
14. Are you flexible and adaptable?
15. Can you think on your feet in situations of chaos and stress?
16. Do you prefer a regular work schedule that is the same every week?
17. Is working out and staying in shape a constant battle for you?
18. Are you afraid of heights or closed-in spaces?
19. Do you have a strong sense of independence?
20. Would you enjoy studying chemistry and physics?
21. Can you handle seeing gory and unpleasant things at work?
22. Are you willing to risk your life to save others?
23. Do you enjoy the thrill of adventure?
24. Do you enjoy experiencing new situations each day?
25. Do you like to play team sports?

If you answered yes to the majority of questions numbered 1–5, 11–15, and 21–25, then you should consider a job in fire suppression. If you answered yes to the majority of questions numbered 6–10, and 16–20, then you may prefer a job in fire prevention or other fire-related services, rather than fire suppression. If you answered yes to all of the questions listed above, you are well-suited for a career in either fire suppression or fire prevention/instruction. However, if you answered no to the majority of the questions above, you may want to reconsider your future in the firefighting field.

INSIDE TRACK

Wayne Williams
Smoke Jumper Foreman
U.S. Forest Service

I've been a firefighter for 26 years—I started working for the California Division of Forestry back in 1974 when I was 18 years old, and I started with the Forest Service in 1975. I worked on a wildland firefighting truck in the Eldorado National Forest outside of Lake Tahoe and started as a smoke jumper in 1977. I've been a smoke jumper since then.

I really like the job a lot—I don't really have any dislikes about it. I feel fortunate to have had this career, and I'll be retiring in six years when I'm 50 with full benefits. I feel lucky. Also I think that structural firefighters have a much more difficult and dangerous job—as wildland firefighters, smoke jumpers don't have to contend with the hazards of working inside of a burning structure.

I work year-round, five days a week, but the schedules vary—when we're on a fire we may be working 16–18 hours a day. We get one mandatory day off every 14 days. Smoke jumpers are unique in that when we're not working a fire, a lot of our time is spent making our equipment—we're all trained in how to manufacture our own parachutes, packs, jumpsuits, and other pieces of equipment.

I think that the job of a smoke jumper has definitely changed for the better since I began. It's much safer, mostly due to technology and training. In addition to the rookie training, every spring we go through a refresher course that lasts for about two weeks.

The main advice I'd give to someone who wants to be a smoke jumper for the Forest Service is to start getting wildland firefighting experience as soon as possible. Technically, you need a couple of seasons of this experience, but in reality the competition may have as many as ten seasons, so you have to get as much as you can. Start out small, with local and state agencies, and start making your way up the ladder.

CHAPTER two

APPLYING FOR THE JOB

THIS CHAPTER gives you the information you need to apply for and land a job as a firefighter in any of the following areas: municipal fire department, state or federal government, the military, or a private fire company. For municipal fire departments, which hire the most firefighters annually, you'll get tips on how to succeed in every portion of the formal application process: the written exam, the physical ability test, the oral interview, the oral board, and much more. You'll get the latest information on how you can use the Internet to land a job as well as how veteran's preference points can boost your application's score.

AS YOU'VE learned, competition for firefighting jobs is stiff. When you find an opening and apply for a position, you will most likely be one of many applicants competing for the same job. Most fire departments put job applicants through a rigorous selection process that can take from several months to a year or more, because they want to find firefighters who will excel on the job. Firefighters need to be smart enough to learn the chemistry, physics, and biology of emergency services; strong enough to carry a person out of a burning building; fit enough to respond to several emergencies in a day, sometimes without sleep; honest enough to be trusted inside every home and business in town; and compassionate and polite enough to interact with the public daily.

What can you do to edge out the competition? The first step is to understand what fire departments are looking for in the candidates they hire. Make sure you have done all you can to make yourself the best job candidate you can be. Then arm yourself with the latest information on the application process. If you know what to expect, you'll be ahead of the competition, who may fail one or more steps in the process simply because they didn't know what was expected.

THE CANDIDATE FIRE DEPARTMENTS WANT TO HIRE

The application process is designed to weed out those who don't have what it takes to work in the fire protection industry and to seek out those who do. While there are many very different steps in the process, they all have that same goal. Generally speaking, fire departments are looking for applicants who

- ▶ have the education required (the minimum is a high school diploma or GED)
- ▶ are stable and secure, with the ability to handle stress
- ▶ conduct themselves appropriately (traffic tickets, misdemeanor charges, drug use, or a poor work record can take an otherwise good candidate out of the running)
- ▶ are in excellent physical condition
- ▶ do not smoke (not required by all departments, but the requirement is on the rise)
- ▶ have experience (with a Fire Explorer program, or a volunteer department)
- ▶ are certified to perform CPR and/or have training as an EMT or paramedic
- ▶ have certification (required by some states) from a fire science training program
- ▶ have acquired more than the minimum required education (by taking college courses or getting a degree in fire science management, hazardous materials, and/or fire protection engineering)

Fire departments can learn about many of the items in the list above by having the prospective firefighter fill out an application and send in documents such as school transcripts. Other criteria are more subjective, and hiring departments use a number of techniques to find suitable applicants. The possible steps in the application process for municipal firefighters follow later in this chapter. Not all of the hiring process steps described are required by every fire department. You can look up the specific requirements for several locations in one of the books mentioned in Appendix C under the heading "Test Prep Materials."

Additional Possible Requirements

▶ testing: drug screening, psychological examination, medical examination, background investigation (which may include checking your personal references, criminal and driving records, and fingerprints), and a polygraph (lie detector) test
▶ proof of residency, voter registration certificate, proof of citizenship (birth certificate, naturalization papers, or baptismal papers), and a valid driver's license
▶ uncorrected vision of at least 20/50 in both eyes; some fire departments require 20/20; others have no uncorrected limits
▶ certification that you have not smoked a cigarette, cigar, or pipe in the past year

PLAN FOR SUCCESS

Now that you have an idea of what is expected of you, you can formulate a plan for success. Whether you are about to enter the field or are still in school with a few years before you begin a job search, there are things you can do right now to get ready for your career in fire protection:

▶ do well in school and get your diploma
▶ begin a lifelong habit of staying in good physical condition

- ▶ stay out of trouble: drinking, drug use, vandalism, stealing, and other illegal behavior could make it hard or impossible for you to have the career of your choice
- ▶ do your best at your current job: show up on time; treat your boss, coworkers, and the public with respect; build a reputation you'll be proud to talk about with your future employer
- ▶ consider enrolling in a Fire Explorer program
- ▶ get involved in your community by volunteering
- ▶ if you are in high school, consider college and/or military service

JUST THE FACTS

Fire Prevention Week, held for one week every October, promotes fire safety programs such as Fire Drills: The Great Escape!, that have resulted in 58 documented saved lives in the past three years. Local fire stations provide materials to the public relating to fire safety during Fire Prevention Week.

MUNICIPAL FIREFIGHTER SELECTION PROCESS

The application process for the position of municipal firefighter includes many steps that are also found in the processes for state, federal, and private fire-fighting company jobs. The steps will be explained in detail only in this section. The selection process goes far beyond merely filling out the application forms, although those application forms can be long and unwieldy. This section will lead you through the entire application process, giving you tips and techniques doing your best and for increasing your chances of getting hired at the end of the process. You can find out how to make the most of each step of the application process before you begin by reading this section, and that way you can stay a step ahead of the competition.

The Exam or Position Announcement

Applying to be a firefighter differs from applying for most other jobs. The differences begin with the exam or position announcement. You rarely see fire department openings advertised in the Help Wanted section of the newspaper. Instead, the city usually starts looking for potential firefighters by means of a special announcement. This announcement will outline the basic qualifications for the position as well as the steps you will have to go through in the selection process. It often tells you some of the duties you will be expected to perform. It may give the date and place of the written exam, which is usually the first step in the selection process.

To get a copy of this announcement, check your public library. You may also get one directly from the fire department or city personnel department. If exams are held irregularly, the fire or personnel department may maintain a mailing list so that applicants can receive an exam announcement the next time an exam is scheduled. If exams are held frequently, you will sometimes simply be told to show up at the exam site on a given day of the week or month. In those cases, you usually get more information about the job and the selection process when you pass the written exam. Study the exam announcement as well as any other material, such as brochures, that the department sends you.

What Is an Eligibility List?

Most fire departments or the city personnel departments that handle the selection process for them establish a list of eligible candidates, ranking them from highest to lowest. This is commonly referred to as the eligibility list. How ranks are determined varies from place to place; sometimes the rank is based solely on the written exam score, sometimes on the physical ability test, and sometimes on a combination of factors. Even if you make it through the entire selection process, the likelihood that you will be hired as a firefighter often depends on your placement on this list, which is determined by the quality of your performance in one or more parts of the selection process.

Make a commitment now: you need to work hard, in advance, to do well on the written exam, the physical ability test, and the oral interview (if there is one), so that your name will stand out at the top of your agency's eligibility list. You should aim to get 100% correct answers on every test to get a chance at coming out toward the top of the list. Some applicants may be getting extra points for living in the jurisdiction or for active military duty, so you need to score very high to compete with them. Often firefighters on waiting lists will have scores of 100–105 due to extra points, so don't plan on merely passing with a score in the 70s or 80s if you want to get called from the eligibility list.

> High test scores are essential to be hired in Fort Worth, Texas. For the group of appli-
> cants who tested on February 16, 2000, the top-ranked test taker scored 104 (with vet-
> eran's preference points). Applicants who had perfect test scores of 100 ranked in the
> top 10. An applicant with a score of 98 was ranked 28, and a test taker who scored 92
> was ranked 103! So a score that might have been considered an A on a test you took
> in school would place you well below the score necessary to get hired in Fort Worth.

The Application

Often the first step in the process of becoming a firefighter is filling out an application. It may be a form that you fill out providing information about your education, employment experience, and personal data; or it may be an application to take the written or the physical test, with the more complete form coming later in the process. In any case, at some point you will proba- bly be asked some questions you wouldn't expect to see on a regular job appli- cation. You might be asked things like whether you've ever gotten any speed- ing tickets or been in trouble with the law, whether you've used illegal drugs, or even whether any relatives work for the city or the fire department. Your answers to these as well as the more conventional questions will serve as the starting point if the department conducts an investigation of your back- ground, so it's important to answer all questions accurately and honestly.

Application Tips

- If you have access to a typewriter, use it; if not, write as legibly as you can.
- Neatness and accuracy count; filling in your apartment number in the blank labeled "city" reflects poorly on your ability to follow directions.
- Verify all information you put on the form. Don't guess or estimate; if you're not sure of the exact address of your high school or what year you worked for a certain company, look it up.
- If you're mailing your application, take care to submit it to the proper address; it

might go to the personnel department rather than to the fire department, so follow directions.

■ Make a copy of your application before sending it in, so you can use it as a guide when filling out additional applications.

Sample Applications

See the sample applications on the following pages to get an idea of what you might be filling out as an initial step in becoming a firefighter. These applications are provided as samples only; they cannot be used to submit to any fire departments. You need to get an original application form from the appropriate department when you're ready to apply. However, you can read through these samples to find out what sort of information you'll be asked to provide and to practice filling out the application. Don't underestimate this step. Filling out the application neatly and accurately can make or break your quest for employment, because it is a key part of the employment process.

The Written Exam

In most jurisdictions, taking a written exam is the next step in the application process. The written exam is your first opportunity to show that you have what it takes to become a firefighter. As such, it's extremely important. People who don't pass the written exam don't go any farther in the selection process. Furthermore, the written exam score often figures into an applicant's rank on the eligibility list; in some cases, this score by itself determines your rank, while in others it is combined with other scores, such as physical ability or oral board scores. The exam bulletin may specify what your rank will be based on.

Written exams for most municipal fire departments test basic skills and aptitudes: how well you understand what you read, your ability to follow directions, your judgment and reasoning skills, your ability to read and understand maps and floor plans, your math skills, and sometimes your memory. In this type of preliminary written exam, you will not be tested on

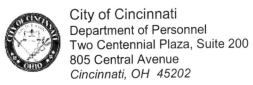

City of Cincinnati
Department of Personnel
Two Centennial Plaza, Suite 200
805 Central Avenue
Cincinnati, OH 45202

An Equal Opportunity Employer

Open to the Public
Application for

_____
Title of position

First Name:	Middle Initial:	Last Name:

Apartment or Box #: Street Address:	Soc. Sec. No.:

City:	State:	Zip:

Day Phone:	Evening Phone:

CIRCLE ONE

Are you at least 18 years of age?	Yes	No
Have you worked for the City of Cincinnati in the last 2 years?	Yes	No
Do you have a valid driver's license? (Show to staff or mail a copy.)	Yes	No
Do you have a professional license or certificate or CDL? (If so, attach a copy.)	Yes	No
Do you request 5 points for being an honorably discharged veteran? (If so, attach a copy of DD 214)	Yes	No
Do you request 10 points for having a service-connected disability of 10% or more? (If so, attach a copy of DD214 and official statement from the Veteran's Administration.)	Yes	No
Have you ever been convicted of any traffic violations or paid any tickets?	Yes	No
Have you ever been convicted of any other local, state, or federal offense?	Yes	No
May we contact your present employer without contacting you first?	Yes	No
Do you request any reasonable accommodation? (If so, attach a Request for Reasonable Accommodation Form.)	Yes	No

Place a check by each item that you have attached to your application.

Copy of Driver's License (if application is mailed)		Work Experience Form(s)	
Reasonable Accommodation Request		Copy of Transcript(s)	
Copy of license or certificate or CDL		Resume	
Other:		Applicant Flow Sheet	
Copy of statement from Veteran's Administration		Copy of DD214	

All information provided by me in support of my application for employment is true and correct to the best of my knowledge. I understand that misrepresentations or omissions may be cause for rejection, or may be cause for subsequent dismissal if I am hired. I hereby authorize any present or former employer, person, firm, corporation or government agency to answer any and all questions and to release or provide any information within their knowledge records. I agree to hold any and all of them blameless and free of any liability for releasing any truthful information that is within their knowledge or records.

Signature: Date:

INITIALS OF PERSONNEL DEPARTMENT STAFF ONLY: DRIVER'S LICENSE SHOWN   YES_____ NO_____
                                                                        CDL SHOWN   YES_____ NO_____

CITY OF HOUSTON
HUMAN RESOURCES DEPARTMENT
P. O. BOX 1562
HOUSTON, TEXAS 77251

An Equal Opportunity Employer

INTERNET EMPLOYMENT APPLICATION
(PER 029 REV 5/99)

You may attach a resume, but you must still complete all questions and items on this application.

Position	PN #	Today's Date (mm/dd/yy)

Last Name, First, Middle	Social Security # Must be verified
Residence Address	Home Phone
CITY STATE ZIP	Alternate Phone

Do you have a legal right to reside and work in the United States of America ? .... ☐ Yes ☐ No
Proof of citizenship or work authorization will be required for employment.

List below any relatives, including those by marriage or adoption, currently employed by the City

Name of Relative	Relationship	Department	Position

Have you ever been employed by the City of Houston? ☐ Yes ☐ No	Department	Position Held	Date of Separation (mm/dd/yy)	Medical Separation? ☐ Yes ☐ No

Check last grade completed	Name of School or Institution Address, City & State	Did You Graduate?	Did You Receive a GED?	Name of School or Institution Address, City & State
1 - 4 ☐ 5 - 8 ☐ 9 - 12 ☐ GED ☐		☐ Yes ☐ No	☐ Yes ☐ No	

Name of Institution	Address, City & State	Did You Graduate?	Month/Year Graduated	Degree or Diploma Received	Major Subject
College		☐Yes ☐No ___Hrs			
College		☐Yes ☐No ___Hrs			
College - Graduate School		☐Yes ☐No ___Hrs			
Other - Vocational, Trade School		☐ Yes ☐No ___Hrs			

Are you an Armed Forces Veteran? ☐ Yes ☐ No   Branch of Service _____

Type of Discharge _____   Date of Service From _____ To _____

Driver's License #_____ License issued by State of _____

What type of license do you have?
☐ Commercial (CDL)   Class: A ☐ B ☐ C ☐   Endorsement _____
☐ Operators   Class: A ☐ B ☐ C ☐
Have you been convicted of DUI or DWI within the past 3 years? ☐ Yes ☐ No
Is your license presently restricted, suspended or revoked? ☐ Yes ☐ No
        If yes, give the reason _____
        the date it began _____ and the date ended (or will end) _____

HR Form 001, April 2000   **Page 1 of 4**

Employment History - Complete with your full employment history. Begin with your current or most recent job and list all past employment below. If more space is needed, attach another sheet(s).

Name of Employer		Supervisor's Name and Title	
Employer's Address City, State, ZIP		Employer's Phone Number	
Your Title:		Final Salary	☐ Full Time ☐ Part Time ☐ Temporary
FROM: (mm/yyyy)	TO: (mm/yyyy)	# of persons supervised	
Your duties: Reason for leaving			

Name of Employer		Supervisor's Name and Title	
Employer's Address City, State, ZIP		Employer's Phone Number	
Your Title:		Final Salary	☐ Full Time ☐ Part Time ☐ Temporary
FROM: (mm/yyyy)	TO: (mm/yyyy)	# of persons supervised	
Your duties: Reason for leaving			

Name of Employer		Supervisor's Name and Title	
Employer's Address City, State, ZIP		Employer's Phone Number	
Your Title:		Final Salary	☐ Full Time ☐ Part Time ☐ Temporary
FROM: (mm/yyyy)	TO: (mm/yyyy)	# of persons supervised	
Your duties: Reason for leaving			

Name of Employer		Supervisor's Name and Title	
Employer's Address City, State, ZIP		Employer's Phone Number	
Your Title		Final Salary	☐ Full Time ☐ Part Time ☐ Temporary
FROM: (mm/yyyy)	TO: (mm/yyyy)	# of persons supervised	
Your duties: Reason for leaving			

Have you ever been dismissed and/or allowed to resign in lieu of discharge? ☐ Yes ☐ No

If yes, specify
the circumstances

If you have indicated in the Employment History Section that you had a gap in employment, were you laid off or dismissed from a position, you may provide further information here:

Have you ever used another name?.. ☐ Yes ☐ No

If yes, specify the name(s)

Have you ever been convicted of a violation of any criminal statute whether felony or misdemeanor?.......... ☐ Yes ☐ No
(Exclude parking violations) If yes, give:

Date (mm/yy)	Conviction For	County & State of Conviction	Disposition

Are you now or have you ever been on any form of parole, probation or deferred adjudication?.............. ☐ Yes ☐ No

If yes, identify what, where, and how long?

Are you able to meet the schedule and attendance requirements of the position for which you are applying?... ☐ Yes ☐ No

Will you work more than 40 hours in a week if required?.. ☐ Yes ☐ No

What date would you be available for work? (mm/dd/yyyy)

Do you speak a foreign language fluently?	☐ Yes ☐ No
If yes, specify language	
Do you read this language? ☐ Yes ☐ No	Do you write this language? ☐ Yes ☐ No

Machine and Equipment Skills	P C Software Skills

Special Qualifications and Skills. Indicate below any experience, skills, licenses or certifications not provided in other parts of this application, that in your opinion, would qualify you for the position you seek.

List below three references (other than relatives).

Name	Phone	Address, City, State & Zip	Relationship

If the job you are applying for requires any of the following, are you willing and able to: (Check only one response for each question)	Yes	No	Not Applicable
Work outside in all types of weather?			
Work with material that causes a lot of dust in the air?			
Work in an awkward or confining work space?			
Work where your clothes get dirty?			
Work in or around areas that have strong odors or vapors?			
Work at heights of up to 100 feet?			
Work in air contaminated areas?			
Work in shifts?			
Work on weekends and holidays?			
Work rotating shifts or irregular hours?			
Work in a stressful or unpleasant setting?			
Work with the public?			
Work with clients and patients?			

May we contact your present employer for a reference?.............................☐ Yes ☐ No

READ CAREFULLY BEFORE SIGNING! By my signature below, I certify, authorize or acknowledge:

- That all the information provided by me in connection with my application, whether on this document or on any attachment, is complete, true and correct. I know that the City will rely upon this information in making a decision to hire me. Consequently, I further understand that any misstatement, falsification, or omission of information will void my application and prevent any further processing. If the City obtains such information after I am hired, I will be subject to termination from my employment with the City.
- For purposes of verification, any persons, organizations, and educational institutions listed on this application or any attachment, as well as the Department of Public Safety in any state in which I am a resident, at any time upon request, may give to officials of the City of Houston any and all information concerning my previous employment, education, experience or other information (including my motor vehicle records) they might have regarding any of the subjects listed on my application. I unconditionally and irrevocably release all such persons, organizations or educational institutions from all liability and damages which may result from providing the information requested to the City.
- That only a representative of the Human Resources Department can make an offer of employment to me, and that such offer is not a contract for a specific term. No one else may offer or promise me anything.
- That upon request, a reasonable accommodation in accordance with the American with Disabilities Act (ADA) will be made for me, in the application process or after I am hired, if, now or in the future, I am disabled.
- That if offered a job, prior to my start date with the City, I will be fingerprinted and that a criminal background check will be conducted.
- That if offered employment with the City of Houston, I must successfully pass a physical examination and a drug test as conditions of employment.

_____   _____
Print Full Name   Social Security Number

_____   _____
Signature   Date (mm/dd/yy)

I learned about this job from the following source: (check 1 only)
1 ☐	City Employee	5 ☐	Texas Workforce Commission	9 ☐	Job Line
2 ☐	Internet	6 ☐	School Referral	10 ☐	Other:
3 ☐	Houston Chronicle	7 ☐	Social Service Agency		
4 ☐	Walk-In	8 ☐	City Job Announcement		

The federal Military Selective Service Act requires males to register for the Selective Service System within 30 days of their 18th birthday. Almost all male U.S. citizens and male aliens living in the U.S. who are 18 through 25 are required to register with Selective Service. Failure to register as required will subject the individual to state and federal penalties.

your knowledge of fire behavior, firefighting procedures, or any other specific body of knowledge. This test is designed only to see if you can read, reason, and do basic math.

In some places, taking the exam involves studying written materials in advance and then answering questions about them on the exam. These written materials generally have to do with fire and fire fighting, but all you have to do is study the guide you're given. You're still being tested just on your reading skills and memory, and there are good reasons for this. Firefighters have to be able to read, understand, and act on complex written materials, not only fire law and fire procedures, but also scientific materials about fire, combustible materials, chemicals, and so forth. An experienced firefighter from Dallas, Texas says:

Indeed, firefighters have to be able to think clearly and independently, because lives depend on decisions they make in a split second. They have to

> Some people think that all you need is physical strength and a hefty dose of courage to become a good firefighter. That is a typical misconception that the public often has about what it takes to become a firefighter. In reality, we have to know a lot about fire and smoke and how they are affected by a building's construction. We have to know how fire travels, what will make it larger, what parts of buildings are the most dangerous, and a lot of other scientific things. In order to gain the necessary knowledge, we undergo training programs on a regular basis. If you don't have basic math, reading, and reasoning skills, you won't be able to cut it as a firefighter.

be able to do enough math to read and understand pressure gauges or estimate the height of a building and the amount of hose needed to reach to the third floor. They have to be able to read maps so they can get to the emergency site quickly, and floor plans, so they can find their way to an exit, even in a smoke-filled building.

Most exams are multiple-choice tests of the sort you've often encountered in school. You get an exam book and an answer sheet where you have to fill in circles or squares with a number 2 pencil. Try the practice test below to familiarize yourself with this format and with the types of questions you will likely be asked.

Applicants are generally notified in writing about their performance on the exam. The notification may simply say whether or not you passed, or it may tell you what your score was. It may also say when you should show up for the next step in the process, which is often the physical ability test.

Written Exam Tips

■ Ask for and use any material the fire department or personnel department publishes about the written test; some agencies have study guides, and some even conduct study sessions.

■ Locate and read test preparation books geared for fire fighting written exams, to increase your score (see Appendix C for a list of useful test preparation books).

■ Prepare by taking many practice tests.

■ Try to find people who have taken the exam recently and ask them about what was on the exam. Their hindsight—"I wish I had studied . . ."—can be your foresight.

Practice Test

This practice test contains questions similar to those you might see on an actual test. It should give you a sense of what you might expect to find on a written exam, but it should not be used to assess whether you are prepared for your actual exam. It only offers a sampling of each question type; it does not include every possible question type. You might also find map-reading, mechanical aptitude, charts and graphs, and other such questions on a written exam. For more test preparation materials, see Appendix C.

Questions about You

These are questions that ask your responses to various situations. In some cases, you may think that different responses are true of you in different situations. You still need to choose the response that seems most like you, most of the time.

These questions are to help us understand you. It is better to be honest about how you would handle a situation than to try to guess how you "should" handle it. If you try to predict what the right answer is supposed to be, you may often be wrong. In addition, you may present an unrealistic, misleading, or inconsistent picture of yourself.

1. When you are talking to someone who has recently been involved in a dangerous situation, such as a car accident, it is better to
    a. get the person to focus on the facts of what happened, rather than talking about his or her feelings
    b. allow the person to talk about his or her feelings while describing what happened
2. When a coworker is having personal problems that are affecting his or her ability to get the job done, it is better to
    a. encourage the person to tell you about his problems so that you can help
    b. let the coworker know that you would be willing to take some of his or her work if it would help
    c. not discuss personal problems at work and let the person work them out for him- or herself
    d. encourage the coworker to talk to someone who can help him or her solve those personal problems
3. When you make decisions, you prefer to
    a. make a decision by yourself, then get input from others before you take action
    b. consider your options, then get input from others before you decide
    c. formulate some ideas to present to others, then let the group decide
    d. discuss your ideas with others to develop options before you decide
4. After someone has explained something new to you, such as during training for a new job, you usually
    a. are able to remember all the information you need
    b. remember most of what you were told
    c. wish you had listened better when it was being explained

Reading Comprehension

Questions 5–8 refer to the following reading passage:

The emotional abilities children acquire in later life build on those of the earliest years, and these abilities are the essential foundation for all learning. Successful learning is not predicted by how many facts a person knows or the ability to read so much as by emotional and social measures: being self-assured and interested;

knowing what kind of behavior is expected and how to rein in the impulse to behave poorly; being able to wait, to follow directions, and to turn to others for help; and expressing needs while getting along with others.

A child's emotional abilities depend on the most basic of all knowledge, how to learn. There are seven key ingredients of this crucial capacity, all related to emotional intelligence:

Confidence. A sense of control and mastery of one's body, behavior, and world; the child's sense that he or she is more likely than not to succeed at what he or she undertakes and that adults will be helpful.

Curiosity. The sense that finding out about things is positive and leads to pleasure.

Intentionality. The wish and capacity to have an impact and to act upon that with persistence. This is related to a sense of competence, of being effective.

Self-Control. The ability to modulate and control one's own actions in age-appropriate ways; a sense of inner control.

Relatedness. The ability to engage with others based on the sense of being understood by and understanding others.

Capacity to Communicate. The wish and ability to verbally exchange ideas, feelings, and concepts with others. This is related to a sense of trust in others and pleasure in engaging with others, including adults.

Cooperativeness. The ability to balance one's own needs with those of others in group activity.

5. According to this passage, which of the following is true?
   a. The ability to read is not important to a child's successful learning.
   b. A child's level of emotional intelligence is highly related to how well the child can control his or her impulses.
   c. Emotional intelligence is learned early in life and does not change once adulthood is reached.
   d. A child's level of emotional intelligence is independent of the child's ability to learn in school.
6. Sara is selling chocolate bars to raise money for the school's new gymnasium. The first ten people she asks refuse to buy any chocolate. According to this passage, she should

a. think of other ways to make money for the new gymnasium instead of continuing to fail.

b. stop trying to sell the chocolate since she has been unsuccessful

c. freely vent her frustration to other students who are selling more candy

d. believe that she will begin to sell more chocolate, if she remains positive and keeps trying

7. A class is attending a science fair at which there are several new scientific inventions. As the children walk past the displays, one of the students, Joseph, talks to the other students about topics not related to the science fair. When he is not talking, he is watching all the people around him. Based on the information in this passage, what do you think about Joseph's behavior?

a. He is balancing his need to socialize with the need to let other students enjoy the science fair.

b. He is lacking self-control, because he does not like the science fair.

c. He seems to lack a natural curiosity and appreciation for learning about new things.

d. He feels understood only if he is talking about himself.

8. A school counselor notices that a young student named Marisha is a loner. She speaks only when someone speaks to her first. During lunch and in classes, she sits by herself. Which of the seven key ingredients for being able to learn does Marisha seem to be missing?

a. confidence

b. curiosity

c. intentionality

d. self-control

e. relatedness

f. capacity to communicate

g. cooperativeness

Writing Skills

The writing skills section of the test may have questions similar to any of the ones below. The format of the questions will vary.

In the examples below numbered 1–4, there are several writing errors. You will find one of these types of errors in each of questions 9–14.

Examples:

1. Grammar Error Example:

Incorrect: The woman has went to the store.

Correct: The woman has gone to the store.

2. Punctuation Error Example:

Incorrect: After reading the book you will write a report.

Correct: After reading the book, you will write a report.

3. Capitalization Error Example:

Incorrect: You should turn left on Main street.

Correct: You should turn left on Main Street.

4. Spelling Error Example:

Incorrect: The two women went into businiss together.

Correct: The two women went into business together.

Questions 9–14. For each line below, identify the type of error (1–4 above), and mark that number on your answer sheet.

9. It is a well-known fact that everyone experiences dreams during sleep. The value and importence of

10. dreams, however—has been debated over the centuries. Nevertheless, many people would like to

11. remember their dreams, but have difficulty doing so. Since many dreams ocur shortly before a person

12. awakes, you can often "Catch" yourself dreaming by setting your alarm for 15 minutes before you normally

13. get up. Your dreams may provide interesting insights into your life. As psychologist Carl Jung has wrote,

14. "The dream is the small hidden door in the deepest, and most intimate sanctum of the soul."

15. Choose the statement below that you think is the most clear, concise, and effective. It should also contain correct grammar, punctuation, and spelling.

    a. A White House Commission have recommended a number of steps, to improve air safety, including fingerprinting all airline employees.

    b. A White House commission recommended a number of steps to improve air safety, one of which would be to fingerprint all Airline Employees.

    c. A White House Commission recommended a number of steps, such as fingerprinting all airline employees to improve Air Safety.

d. A White House commission has recommended a number of steps to improve air safety, including FBI checks of fingerprints of all airline employees.

In the following question, fill in the blank with the correct word or phrase.

16. Joe, Bill, and "_____" decided to go to the meeting together.

    a. us

    b. me

    c. I

    d. them

Mathematical Skills

You will not be allowed to use a calculator on the test.

17. What is the decimal equivalent of 6/15?

    a. .25

    b. 30

    c. 35

    d. 40

18. A piece of rope is 50 feet in length. It is found that the rope shrank by 10% when it got wet. After drying, the rope was stretched 5% longer than its wet length. How long is the rope after it is stretched?

    a. 57.50 feet

    b. 55.00 feet

    c. 47.50 feet

    d. 47.25 feet

Situational Questions

These questions measure a variety of skills, including problem solving, decision making, and judgment, as well as many other relevant skills. Try to place yourself in each situation, or remember a situation you have been in that was similar to the one described, and choose the response (or responses) that you think best. If none of the answers is exactly what you would do or what you think would be best, choose the answer (or answers) that comes closest to how you feel or think.

19. Lately you have noticed an increase in salespeople coming to your door trying to sell you various items. You find this irritating, and you wish they would stop. What is the best way to solve this problem? Choose two answers.

    a. Let the salespeople tell you about their products before deciding whether you are interested.

    b. Politely tell each salesperson that you are not interested in buying anything.

    c. Angrily tell each salesperson to leave you alone.

    d. Refuse to open your door to anyone who looks like a salesperson.

    e. Put up a sign on your door that says "No Solicitors."

    f. Let the salespeople believe that they are close to making a sale, then tell them to leave.

20. You are attending a playoff game for your university basketball team, the Tigers. They are playing the Elks. As you go to get a hot dog, you accidentally bump into an Elks fan. Even though you apologize, he turns to you and yells: "What's the matter with you, you idiot? You better look where you're going, you stupid Tiger fan. Where'd you get that stupid hat? All you stupid Tiger fans are wearing those stupid hats. Those hats are stupid and you're stupid!" You do not feel threatened by the man, but you think he is irritating. Of the following, which would you be most likely to say? Choose three answers.

    a. "You're the one who's acting stupid here."

    b. "Excuse me. I'm going back to my seat now."

    c. "Like I said, I'm sorry I bumped into you."

    d. "Move away from me please."

    e. "I'm just here to have fun at the game."

    f. "Security can kick you out of here for bothering people."

    g. "Why don't we just go back to our seats and enjoy the game."

    h. "Hey man, let's forget the insults."

    i. "No wonder everyone thinks Elks fans are a bunch of hotheads."

21. You are going to move out of a house after renting it for three years. The house is in good condition. When the landlord inspects the house, he says that you will have to paint the inside of the house or he will keep your security deposit. You have called the local housing authority and have found out that painting is your landlord's responsibility. When you tell him this, he still disagrees. What do you do?

    a. Do the painting yourself, and insist on getting your deposit back.

    b. Tell him that you will pursue the matter legally.

    c. Offer to pay for half of the painting if he will give you your deposit back.

    d. Give up on getting your deposit back, because it is not worth the fight.

Answers to the Practice Test

Questions about You

Questions 1–4 ask you to answer honestly how you would respond in these situations. Therefore there is no "right" answer. Your honest answers allow the fire department to learn about who you are, one of the important purposes of the written exam.

Reading Comprehension

5. **b.** is correct because self-control is one of the emotional skills listed in the passage.
6. **d.** is correct. Sara is demonstrating intentionality by believing that she can sell more chocolate.
7. **c.** is correct. Based on Joseph's behavior, it is not clear if any of the other statements are true.
8. **f.** is correct. Marisha clearly has trouble communicating with others. She may also lack confidence or relatedness, but we can't tell that for sure from her behavior.

Writing Skills

9. **4.** is correct. The word *importance* is misspelled.
10. **2.** is correct. The punctuation of "however—has" is incorrect. The correct punctuation is "however, has."
11. **4.** is correct. The word *occur* is misspelled.
12. **3.** is correct. The word *catch* should not be capitalized.
13. **1.** is correct. "Jung wrote," is correct, not "has wrote."
14. **2.** is correct. There should not be a comma between "deepest" and "and most."
15. **d.** is correct. The other options all have at least one punctuation or capitalization error. In addition, choice 4 provides the information in the most concise yet complete way.
16. **c.** is correct.

Mathematical Skills

17. **d.** is correct. To solve this problem, divide 6 by 15.
18. **d.** is correct. To solve this problem, first multiply 50 by .10. This is equal to 5. Next, subtract 5 from 50. The result is 45. Then multiply 45 by .05. This is equal to 2.25. Lastly, add 2.25 to 45.

Situational Questions

19. **b.** and **e.** are the best choices. Did you remember to choose two answers?
20. **b.**, **c.**, and **g.** are the best choices. Did you choose three answers?

21. **b.** is the best choice. In this case, the landlord is breaking the law. Telling him your intention gives him the opportunity to change his mind.

The Physical Ability Test

The physical ability test is the next step in the process for many fire departments. You may be asked to bring a note from your doctor saying that you are in good enough shape to undertake the physical ability test before you will be allowed to participate. This should be an indication that you should expect the test to be tough. Firefighting is, after all, physically demanding work. Lives depend on whether your strength, stamina, and overall fitness allow you to carry out the necessary tasks during an emergency. If you make it to the academy and later into a fire company, you can expect to continue physical training and exercises throughout your career. In fact, some cities require all firefighters to retake the physical ability test every year.

The exact events that make up the physical ability test vary from place to place, but the tasks you have to perform are almost always job related, they're a lot like the physical tasks you will actually have to perform as a firefighter. Many times the test is set up like an obstacle course, and it is timed, with a cut-off time for passing. Often you have to wear full, heavy protective gear, including an air pack, throughout these events. Here's an example of the events in a test that you would typically have five to seven minutes to complete:

- ▶ dummy drag
- ▶ hose drag
- ▶ stair climb
- ▶ tunnel climb
- ▶ ladder raise and climb
- ▶ wall jump

In an obstacle course setup like this one, you might be given the opportunity to walk the course before you actually have to take the test. Take advantage of the walk-through. In departments where the physical ability test figures into your rank on the eligibility list, merely meeting the maximum time to pass isn't good enough; people who have faster times will be higher on the list than you are. You can usually find out just what tasks are included in the physical ability test from the exam announcement or related materials.

Different departments have varying policies on retesting if you fail. Some allow you to retest on the same day after a rest period. Some allow you to come back another time and try again, usually up to a set maximum number of tries. In some departments, your first try is the only chance you get; if you fail, you're out, at least until the next testing period. Not many departments will allow you to retest, if you have already passed, simply to better your time.

A prospective firefighter from Palm Harbor, Florida, has this to say about the physical ability tests:

All physical ability tests are different, depending on the fire department's equipment and course setup. I've taken physical ability tests for five different municipal fire departments in the last year and a half, and some were much harder than others. Don't be fooled into thinking all physical tests are easy if you happen to take one that doesn't seem very difficult. The next one might be a killer. I'm in great shape, but I just took a test that was a lot harder than the four I'd taken previously. My advice is to do a lot of running to prepare for physical ability tests, because the tough tests really take a lot of endurance.

Many urban fire departments report that the physical ability test is the one step of the process in which the most applicants fail. People come in unprepared; they're simply not strong enough or fast enough to do all the events, while wearing heavy gear, in the time allotted. Female applicants in particular have high failure rates on physical ability tests because some of the events require a lot of upper-body strength.

Be assured that the physical ability test is one area where advance preparation is almost guaranteed to pay off. No matter what your physical condition is, start or continue an exercise program now. You can design your program around the requirements listed in the exam announcement, although any exercise that increases your strength and stamina will help. Because sheer brute force is required to drag a 150-pound dummy or to lift a 50-foot ladder, exercises that increase your strength are particularly important. But you'll also want to include some aerobic exercise such as running or swimming, to improve your stamina and overall fitness as well.

If you're not in great shape, consult a doctor before you begin an exercise program. Start slowly and increase your activity as you go. As you gain strength, start wearing weights on your ankles and wrists, and later add a weighted backpack. To stay motivated, consider working out with a partner; not only is this more fun, but it also helps guard against the temptation to cheat by skipping a day or doing fewer "reps."

Physical Ability Exam Tips

- Take advantage of any training sessions or test course walk-throughs the fire department offers; their sole purpose is to help you pass the physical test.
- Start exercising immediately; work on aerobic conditioning and strength training, concentrating on the upper body.
- If you smoke, stop.
- If you're overweight, begin to eat a healthier diet designed to help you lose weight.
- Stay motivated: exercise with a friend, listen to music while working out, give yourself rewards for reaching milestones like shaving a minute off your mile run time or bench-pressing 10 more pounds.

The Background Investigation

Firefighters must be citizens of good character who can get along with both their company and the people they serve. A background investigation is one of the ways a hiring department determines whether an applicant is the kind of person it is looking for. Not all fire departments conduct background investigations, but the ones that do conduct them only on applicants who have passed the written and physical tests.

You may not be alerted that an investigation is taking place, so be sure to answer everything on your application honestly. If your friends, classmates, coworkers, or family give information that contradicts what you've said, you may be dropped from the application process.

Some departments will investigate you in great depth, asking their contacts how long and how well they knew you and what kind of person they found you to be. Did you meet your obligations? How did you deal with problems? Did they find you to be an honest person? Do they know of anything that might affect your fitness to be a firefighter? The references you provided will lead the investigator to other people who knew you, and when the investigator is finished, he or she will have a more complete picture of the kind of person you are. Other fire departments conduct a fairly superficial check, calling your former employers and schools simply to verify the information you provided and to ask some basic questions about your conduct.

A few fire departments include a polygraph, or lie detector test as part of the background investigation. As long as you've been honest throughout the application process, a lie detector test should not cause you concern. The test is designed to pick up physical changes that occur under stress, as when someone is lying. Nervousness about the test experience is expected, and the test is designed to compensate for the ordinary stress people feel when taking a polygraph test. The test taker asks you a few simple questions before beginning, such as "What is your name?" to establish your baseline response.

The best way to improve your chances of successfully getting through a background investigation is to clean up any previous problems that might give you trouble. You can't change the past, but you can use the present to improve your chances in the future. Pay your old traffic tickets, get that juvenile offense that the lawyer said wouldn't count officially expunged from your record, document your full recovery from a serious illness or your drug-free status since high school. Be prepared to answer honestly about your past mistakes, while showing how you have risen above them and moved on.

The Oral Interview and Selection Board

The selection process in most fire departments includes one or more oral interviews. In some cities, applicants who get this far in the process meet with the fire chief or deputy fire chief, who may conduct something like a regular job interview. A recent Seattle fire department job listing described the interview as including "a discussion of the candidate's education, employment experience, military background, driving history, traffic citations, misdemeanor and/or felony convictions, and other related skills and qualifications." In the interview process, the chief will also be assessing your interpersonal skills, whether you seem honest and relatively comfortable in talking to him or her.

You may face an oral selection board in addition to or in place of your interview with the chief. An oral board is similar to a job interview with a fire chief in that you are asked to answer questions so an assessment can be made about your interpersonal skills, communication skills, judgement and decision-making abilities, respect for diversity, and adaptability. The board consists of two to five people, who may be firefighters, civilian personnel, and/or interview specialists. There is usually some variety in the makeup of the board, which may include officers of various ranks and civilians from the personnel department or from the community.

The way the interview is conducted depends on the practices of the individual department. You may be asked a few standard questions, such as "Why do you want to be a firefighter?" "What qualities do you have that would make you good at this job?" and "Could you describe in detail your physical exercise program?" You may be asked about your background, especially if your application or background investigation raised any questions in the board members' minds. Have answers prepared for any questions you can think of that would be asked about your background, in case they come up during the board interview.

Instead of or in addition to such questions, you may be presented with hypothetical situations to which you will be asked to respond. Situational questions involve circumstances common in fighting fires. A board member may say something like: "After a dwelling fire is under control, you're walking through the building checking its structural soundness. When you walk into the living room, you see a fellow firefighter sticking a gold watch into the pocket of his coat. What would you do?" You would then have to come up with an appropriate response to this situation.

Increasingly, cities have standardized the oral board questions. The same questions are asked of every candidate, and when the interview is over the board rates each candidate on a standard scale. This procedure helps the interviewers reach a somewhat more objective conclusion about the candidates they have interviewed and may result in a score that is included in the factors used to rank candidates in the eligibility list.

A career firefighter from California has this advice to give prospective firefighters who complete an oral interview or an oral board:

As soon as you leave, take out a pen and paper and write down as many of the questions asked during the session as you can remember. Then, think about your responses to the questions and how you could make them better. Take time to synthesize your responses to those questions and come up with additional ways you can respond in the future. Chances are that you'll be asked similar questions in another interview. This way you can prepare ahead of time for the next interview or oral board that you'll face.

How to Prepare for the Oral Board or Interview

If the fire department you're applying to hands out any material about the oral board, study it carefully. It may tell you what the board is looking for. It may even give you some sample questions you can practice with.

Whether you're facing an oral board or an individual interview, think about your answers to questions you might be asked. You might even try to write your own oral board questions and situations, and write down your answers if you want to. Practice saying them in front of a mirror until you feel comfortable, but don't memorize them. You don't want to sound like you're reciting from a book. Your answers should sound conversational even though you've prepared in advance.

Then enlist friends or family to serve as a mock oral board or interviewer. If you know a practised public speaker, or someone with interviewing expertise, get him or her to help. Give them your questions, tell them about what you've learned, and then have a practice oral board or interview. Start from the moment you walk into the room. Go through the entire session as if it were the real thing, and then ask your mock board or interviewer for feedback on your performance. It may even help to videotape your mock board session. The camera can reveal things about your body language or habits that you don't even know about.

Oral Board or Interview Tips

- Dress neatly and conservatively, as you would for a business interview.
- Be polite; say "please" and "thank you," "sir" and "ma'am."
- Look at board members or interviewers as they speak to you, and listen carefully to what they say.
- Think before you speak; nod or say "okay" to indicate that you understand the question, and then pause for a moment to collect your thoughts before speaking.
- Take a deep breath, relax, and count to five to regain composure if you become nervous.

The Psychological Evaluation

Some cities include a psychological evaluation as part of the firefighter selection process. The fire department wants to make sure that you are emotionally and mentally stable before putting you in a high-stress job in which you have to interact with peers, superiors, and the public. The psychological evaluation is not designed to uncover your deep, dark secrets; its only purpose is to make sure you have the mental and emotional health to do the job.

If your fire department has a psychological evaluation, most likely that means you'll be taking one or two written tests. A few cities have candidates interviewed by a psychologist or a psychiatrist. If you have to take a written psychological test, it is likely to be a standardized multiple-choice or true-false test licensed from a psychological testing company. The Minnesota Multiphasic Personality Inventory (MMPI) is one commonly used test. Such tests typically ask you about your interests, attitudes, and background. They may take one hour or several; the hiring agency will let you know approximately how much time to allot.

If you need to undergo an oral psychological assessment, you'll meet with a psychologist or a psychiatrist, who may be on the hiring agency's staff or an independent contractor. The psychologist may ask you questions about your schooling and jobs, your relationships with family and friends, your habits, and your hobbies. The psychologist may be as interested in the way you answer—whether you come across as open, forthright, and honest—as in the answers themselves.

Don't try to psych out the assessment. The psychologists who designed the written test know more about psyching out tests than you do. They designed the test so that one answer checks against another, to find out whether test takers are lying. Be sure to answer every question openly and honestly, and this part of the process should go smoothly.

The Medical Examination

Before passage of the Americans with Disabilities Act (ADA), many fire departments conducted a medical examination early in the selection process, before the physical ability test. Now, the ADA says it is illegal to do any medical examinations or ask any questions that could reveal an applicant's disability until after a conditional offer of employment has been made. That means that in most jurisdictions you will get such a conditional offer before you are asked to submit to a medical exam.

One exception is the test for use of illegal drugs, which can be administered before a conditional offer of employment. Because firefighters have to be in excellent physical shape and because they are in a position of public trust, the fire department expects you to be drug free. You may have to undergo drug testing periodically throughout your career as a firefighter.

You should know, however, that almost any disability is grounds for disqualification as a firefighter, even under the protections provided by the ADA. Fire fighting requires a high level of physical and mental fitness, and a host of disabilities could prevent a firefighter from fulfilling essential job functions. For instance, a skin condition that requires a man to wear facial hair would disqualify that man from being a firefighter, because facial hair interferes with the proper operation of firefighters' breathing apparatus.

What the Medical Exam Is Like

The medical exam is a thorough physical. The doctor may be on the staff of the hiring agency or someone outside the department with his or her own medical practice. Your blood pressure, temperature, weight, and height will be measured. Your heart and lungs will be listened to and your limbs examined. The doctor will peer into your eyes, ears, nose, and mouth. Your vision and hearing will be tested. Blood and urine will be collected for testing. Because of these tests, you won't know the results of the physical exam right away. You will be notified of the results in writing after the test results come in.

The Waiting Game

You went through the whole process, passed all the tests, did the best you could, and made the eligibility list. The next step is to wait. The Houston Fire Department's application process takes three months, for example, and candidates can wait for a year until their names come up on the eligibility list.

While you are waiting, why not do something to prepare for what you hope is your new career? Do some networking. Talk to firefighters about what the job is really like. Find out if your fire department offers volunteer opportunities or a cadet program. Take a course in first aid or enroll in an EMT program. Even if you don't get called, and even if your rank on the eligibility list doesn't get you a job this time, you'll be better qualified for the next try.

Even though you might be very curious to learn about your standing in the application process, you should resist the temptation to call the fire department for updates about the eligibility list or your chance of getting hired. You might come across as a nuisance to the very people you need to impress; even though you will most likely be talking to a receptionist, you always want to create a good impression with all the people that you come in contact with at the fire department. Many departments have websites or other means of keeping applicants informed about their status. Be sure that you know the correct procedure for obtaining information and follow it. You will demonstrate that you know how to follow protocol, a very important trait for a firefighter.

If at First You Don't Succeed, Part One

The selection process for firefighters is a rigorous one. If you fail one of the steps or do poorly on one of the exams, take time for some serious self-evaluation, so you can do better the next time around. Here are some tips on how you can evaluate your performance on the different steps of the application process.

The Written Test

If you didn't pass the written test, examine the reasons why you didn't do well. Was it just that the format was unfamiliar? Next time, you will know what to expect. Do you need to brush up on some of the skills tested? There are many books designed to help people with basic skills. You might start with the LearningExpress Skill Builder books. (See Appendix C for a list of other helpful texts.) Enlist a teacher or a friend to help you or check out the inexpensive courses offered by local high schools and community colleges. Some fire departments allow you to retest after a waiting period, a period you can use to improve your skills. If the exam isn't being offered again for years, consider trying a different jurisdiction.

The Physical Ability Test

If you don't pass the physical test, your course of action is clear. Increase your daily physical exercise until you know you can do what is required, and then retest or try another jurisdiction.

The Oral Board or Interview

If you don't pass the oral board or interview, try to figure out what the problem was. Do you think your answers were good but perhaps you didn't express them well? Then you need some practice in oral communication. You can take courses or enlist your friends to help you practice.

Did the questions and situations surprise you, so you gave what now seem like inappropriate answers? Then spend time practicing answering similar questions for the next time. Talk to candidates who were successful and ask them what they said. Talk with firefighters you know about what might have been good answers for the questions you were asked. Even if your department doesn't allow you to redo the oral board, you can use what you learn when applying to another fire department.

The Medical Exam

If the medical exam eliminates you, you will usually be notified as to what condition caused the problem. Many conditions are correctable.

Other Reasons

If you don't make the eligibility list and aren't told why, the problem might have been the oral board, the psychological evaluation, or the background investigation. Think of what in your past might lead to questions about your fitness to be a firefighter. Could any of your personal traits or attitudes raise such questions? Is there anything you can do to change these aspects of your past or your personality? If so, you might have a chance when you reapply or apply to another department. If not, you may want to consider another profession.

If you feel you were wrongly excluded on the basis of a psychological evaluation or a background check, most departments have appeals procedures. However, that word *wrongly* is very important. The psychologist or the background investigator almost certainly had to supply a rationale in recommending that the department not hire you. Do you have solid factual evidence that you can use in an administrative hearing to counter such a rationale? If not, you'd be wasting your time and money, as well as the hiring agency's, by making an appeal. Move carefully and get legal advice before you take such a step.

If at First You Don't Succeed, Part Two

If you make the eligibility list, go through the waiting game, and finally aren't selected, don't despair. Think through all the steps of the selection process again and use them to do a critical self-evaluation. Maybe your written, physical, and oral board scores were high enough to pass but not high enough to put you at the top of the list. At the next testing, make sure you're better prepared.

Maybe you had excellent scores that should have put you at the top of the list, and you suspect that you were passed over for someone lower down. That means someone less well qualified was selected while you were not, right? Perhaps. There were probably a lot of people on the list, and a lot of them might have scored high. One more point on a test might have made the difference, or maybe the department had the freedom to pick and choose on the basis of other qualifications. Maybe, in comparison with you, a lot of people on the eligibility list had more education or experience.

There might have been plenty of certified EMTs or paramedics on the list, and they got first crack at the available jobs. It is also possible that members of minority groups and veterans might have been given preference in hiring. Whether or not you think that's fair, you can be assured that it was a conscious decision on the part of the hiring agency; it might even have been mandated from above.

Don't get discouraged. Realize that it may take several tries before you land your dream job. There's a lot of competition out there and not enough openings for everyone to land a job the first time around. Many firefighters have had to persevere for several years before landing a job. A firefighter in Colorado says:

> It took me a lot of time to get on—almost five years, and I had a lot of experience behind me. You need to continually update your education and work on your oral skills. I know people who tried for eight years before they finally made it. It's all worth it in the end. My department just hired a 31-year-old man who has been trying to land a full-time paid position since he was 23, so you can see that it takes time. You have to be patient.

This firefighter's experience is by no means unique. Many firefighters who were recently hired say that it took them a long time to make it into the department they wanted. In fact, a firefighter in California says:

> I was recently hired as a firefighter/paramedic with the American Rural Fire Protection District in California. Getting this job was a dream come true. I have been testing for over four years, taking classes, and volunteering my time, but I feel that it has all been worth it. I love my job, and I plan to stay in this department until I retire.

STATE OR FEDERAL WILDLAND
FIREFIGHTER SELECTION PROCESS

The selection process for finding new firefighters for state and federal government agencies is usually shorter and less involved than the municipal selection process. Another difference is that the selection process is on a much larger scale, since state and federal agencies normally need to hire a much larger group of firefighters than each local government agency does. Also, most wildland firefighter positions are seasonal, so there tends to be significant turnover in the ranks.

While each state and federal agency has its own selection process, there are some things they have in common. You normally have to pass a physical ability test. For example, a state agency located in Idaho requires candidates to take two physical tests: one test requires applicants to run a mile and a half in 11 minutes; the second test requires applicants to run for three miles with a 45-pound-pack on their back within 45 minutes. Many state and federal agencies also require that a short firefighter training course be completed. These training courses may last anywhere from a few hours to a few days to a week or more.

After being hired, wildland firefighters normally need to pass a one-week training course in fighting wildland fires. Applicants who have not yet been hired can also take the training course, but they need to sign a waiver relieving the training company of responsibility if they have any physical problems during the training course. Most week-long training courses offer students what is commonly referred to as a "pink card" or "red card," a small card that wildland firefighters carry with them that specifies their firefighting qualifications.

IN THE NEWS

The summer of 2000 saw the worst wildfire season in history. More than 6.9 million acres of land burned throughout the United States. The fire service relied on over 300 firefighters, half a dozen helicopters, four fire engines, seven bulldozers, and thirteen excavation machines to combat the fires.

How to Apply

For jobs with state agencies, begin your search on the Internet, with the listing for the department of natural resources or the forest service in the state(s) you are interested in working in. There are also employment opportunities listed on www.geocities.com/Yosemite/Gorge/5561/state.html. Associations such as the National Association of State Fire Marshals (NASFM) and the National Association of State Foresters may also be good sources of information.

Most federal jobs are offered through the Office of Personnel Management (OPM). You can visit its website (www.usajobs.opm.gov/a6.htm) and search for firefighting jobs by typing in the Standard Occupational Series Code #0462. A recent search at this site listed openings with the U.S. Forest Service (Department of Agriculture); Bureau of Indian Affairs, National Park Service, Bureau of Land Management, and Fish and Wildlife Service (all Department of the Interior); and the Field Operating Office of the Secretary of the Army and the Air Force Personnel Center (both Department of Defense). For all federal positions, you may apply using the Application for Federal Employment, the Optional Application for Federal Employment (OF-612), or a resume that includes all the information requested by the publication entitled *Applying for a Federal Job* (OF-512). Application procedures are detailed on the OPM's website. Appendix B lists all the federal agencies that hire firefighters, with contact information.

The U.S. Forest Service (USFS) operates regional offices throughout the country that may be contacted for job opportunities. Check the list below for the office(s) near where you'd like to work, and call or write for more information.

USFS NORTHERN REGION (R-1)

Federal Building
PO Box 7669
Missoula, MT 59807
406-329-3511

USFS ROCKY MOUNTAIN REGION (R-2)

740 Simms Street
PO Box 25127
Lakewood, CO 80225
303-275-5350

USFS SOUTHWESTERN REGION (R-3)

Federal Building

517 Gold Avenue SW

Albuquerque, NM 87102

505-842-3292

USFS INTERMOUNTAIN REGION (R-4)

Federal Building

324 25th Street

Ogden, UT 84401

(801-625-5352

USFS PACIFIC SOUTHWEST REGION (R-5)

1323 Club Drive

Vallejo, CA 94592

707-562-8737

USFS PACIFIC NORTHWEST REGION (R-6)

333 SW First Avenue

PO Box 3623

Portland, OR 97208

503-808-2931

USFS SOUTHERN REGION (R-8)

1720 Peachtree Road NW

Atlanta, GA 30367

404-347-2384

USFS EASTERN REGION (R-9)

310 West Wisconsin Avenue, Room 500

Milwaukee, WI 53203

414-297-3600

USFS ALASKA REGION (R-10)

PO Box 21628

Juneau, AK 99802

907-586-8863

USFS NORTHEASTERN AREA—S&PF

5 Radnor Corporate Center, Suite 200

PO Box 6775

Radnor, PA 19087

610-975-4111

For seasonal temporary positions, the best times to inquire are during the months of December and January. Contact a Bureau of Land Management, Forest Service, or National Park Service Human Resources Office closest to the location in which you want to work; or look for openings listed on the OPM Website.

Sample Application

See the sample application on pages 73–74 to get an idea of what you might be filling out as an initial step in becoming a federal firefighter. This application is provided as a sample only and cannot be used to submit for a job. You need to get an original application form from the appropriate department when you're ready to apply. However, you can read through the sample to find out what sort of information you'll be asked to provide and to practice filling out the application. Don't underestimate this step. Filling out the application neatly and accurately can make or break your quest for employment, because it's a key part of the employment process.

MILITARY FIREFIGHTER SELECTION PROCESS

If you would like to go the military route to becoming a firefighter, you need to join the military as the first step of the selection process. You'll need to meet the basic requirements for entering the military (see Chapter 1 for a list of minimum requirements). The next step is to talk to military recruiters to find out how you can get a guarantee of being trained and placed in the fire protection field within the military. You must meet a number of specific requirements in order to qualify for a guaranteed firefighter career area; check with your local recruiting agent to find out exactly what steps you need to take.

The Armed Services Vocational Aptitude Battery (ASVAB)

Many high schools and post-secondary schools offer the ASVAB test to students. It is also offered at various locations nationwide by the military itself. Ask your local recruiter when and where you can take this test. But before you take the test, be sure to prepare for it. You need to achieve a score of 39 or higher on this test in order to be eligible for a firefighting career. There are several test preparation books that lead you through the test step by step and give you plenty of practice taking sample tests. See Appendix C for helpful test preparation books that you can use to increase your score on the all-important ASVAB test.

The Enlistment Agreement

If you achieve a high enough score on the ASVAB test and pass all other requirements, the branch of the military you want to work in may guarantee in writing that your career area will be within the fire protection field as a part of your enlistment agreement. Be sure you read the entire enlistment agreement very carefully and ask any questions that you have before you sign it. It is a legally binding document, so don't sign it without serious thought.

You'll also need to decide the length of your enlistment before you sign on the dotted line. If you plan to leave the military to join a municipal fire department as soon as possible, then you'll want to enlist for the shortest possible time while gaining the most experience you can.

Military Training

After you enlist in the military, you'll undergo basic training for several weeks. If you have fire protection guaranteed as your career area, you'll then be given additional training as a firefighter before being assigned to a military fire department or base.

The Navy offers certified apprenticeship programs for some specialties within the firefighting occupation. The Air Force offers a 13-week fire protection training program at the Goodfellow Air Force Base in San Angelo, Texas, for military members who will be serving as firefighters in the Marines, the Army, or the Air Force. You may be able to achieve college credit for some of your training courses from the Community College of the Air Force.

Form Approved
OMB No. 3206-0219

OPTIONAL APPLICATION FOR FEDERAL EMPLOYMENT - OF 612

ou may apply for most jobs with a resume, this form, or other written format. If your resume or application does not provide all the
ormation requested on this form and in the job vacancy announcement, you may lose consideration for a job.

Job title in announcement	2 Grade(s) applying for	3 Announcement number
Last name	First and middle names	5 Social Security Number - -
Mailing address		7 Phone numbers (include area code) Daytime ( )
City	State ZIP Code	Evening ( )

ORK EXPERIENCE

Describe your paid and nonpaid work experience related to the job for which you are applying. Do **not** attach job descriptions.

Job title (if Federal, include series and grade)

From (MM/YY)	To (MM/YY)	Salary per	Hours per week
		$	
Employer's name and address			Supervisor's name and phone number ( )

Describe your duties and accomplishments

Job title (if Federal, include series and grade)

From (MM/YY)	To (MM/YY)	Salary per	Hours per week
		$	
Employer's name and address			Supervisor's name and phone number ( )

Describe your duties and accomplishments

9 May we contact your current supervisor?

YES   NO Ë   If we need to contact your current supervisor before making an offer, we will contact you first.

EDUCATION

10 Mark highest level completed. **Some HS**   HS/GED   Associate   Bachelor   Master   Doctoral

11 Last high school (HS) or GED school. Give the school's name, city, State, ZIP Code (if known), and year diploma or GED received.

12 Colleges and universities attended. Do **not** attach a copy of your transcript unless requested.

Name			Total Credits Earned		Major(s)	Degree	Year
1)			Semester	Quarter		(if any)	Received
City	State	ZIP Code -					
2)							
		-					
3)							
		-					

OTHER QUALIFICATIONS

13 **Job-related** training courses (give title and year). **Job-related** skills (other languages, computer software/hardware, tools, machinery, typing speed, etc. **Job-related** certificates and licenses (current only). **Job-related** honors, awards, and special accomplishments(publications, memberships in professional/honor societies, leadership activities, public speaking, and performance awards.) Give dates, but do **not** send documents unless requested.

GENERAL

14 Are you a U.S. citizen?   YES   NO   Give the country of your citizenship. _____

15 Do you claim veterans' preference?   NO   YES   Mark your claim of 5 or 10 points below.

5 points   Attach your DD 214 or other proof.   **10 points**   Attach an *Application for 10-Point Veterans' Preference* (SF 15) and proof required.

16 Were you ever a Federal civilian employee?

	Series	Grade	From (MM/YY)	To (MM
NO YES For highest civilian grade give:				

17 Are you eligible for reinstatement based on career or career-conditional Federal status?

NO   YES   If requested, attach SF 50 proof.

APPLICANT CERTIFICATION

18 **I certify** that, to the best of my knowledge and belief, all of the information on and attached to this application is true, correct, complete and made in good faith. **I understand** that false or fraudulent information on or attached to this application may be grounds for not hiring me or firing me after I begin work, and may be punishable by fine or imprisonment. **I understand** that any information I give may be investigated.

SIGNATURE   DATE SIGNED

PRIVATE COMPANY FIREFIGHTER SELECTION PROCESS

Private fire companies are the newest employers within the fire protection field. There are two types of private fire companies: large corporations that employ their own firefighters to protect their equipment on-site and companies that offer fire protection service to a number of clients or in a specific geographic area. Private fire companies offer their services only when and where they are contracted by others to do so.

Companies with On-Site Firefighters

There are hundreds of large companies that hire firefighters or other fire protection specialists to work on-site to protect the company's equipment and other assets. Due to the size and high cost of the equipment at these companies, it's worth the expense of hiring an on-site crew to manage their fire prevention and suppression program. Some examples of companies that hire on-site firefighters or who contract with private fire companies to obtain on-site firefighters are Port Columbus International Airport in Columbus, Ohio; the Federal Express National Operations Center in Memphis, Tennessee; the Hughes Missile System in Arizona; and Boeing, which has several locations and subsidiaries nationwide.

Below is a sample job description from a private company looking for a fire protection specialist:

Fire Protection Engineer

Job Code 23630

The fundamental reason this classification exists is to review building plans and inspect existing structures to ensure conformance to fire protection codes and standards and to assist in writing and updating fire protection codes. Incumbents analyze industrial, commercial and public buildings and other structures before and after construction; evaluate the fire resistance of structures, taking into consideration the usage and contents of building; evaluate the availability of water supplies and water delivery; and evaluate entrance/exit capabilities. Responsibilities include making recommendations for changes in design, materials, or equipment, such as structural components protection, fire protection equipment, alarm systems, and fire-extinguishing devices and systems. Work involves considerable coordination with the Fire Department, Development Services Department, and other departments regarding the development and enforcement of fire protection codes. Some positions may be assigned supervisory responsibility over clerical and professional employees. Work is accomplished with considerable independence within broad policy outlines and is reviewed through evaluation of reports and conferences by a Deputy Fire Chief, Assistant Fire Chief, or Fire Chief.

Essential Functions

- provide technical assistance to architects, contractors, and other private industry personnel in interpreting and complying with fire codes and standards
- recommend changes in fire codes
- review construction site plans and building plans for compliance with fire protection codes and standards
- evaluate the fire resistance of building and structures
- determine whether water availability and water delivery systems are adequate to protect buildings
- demonstrate continuous effort to improve operations, decrease turnaround times, streamline work processes, and work cooperatively and jointly to provide quality seamless customer service

Required Knowledge, Skills, and Abilities

Knowledge of

- building construction, design, and materials as related to fire prevention and fire control
- fire codes and regulations
- fire detection, fire alarm, and fire suppression systems

Ability to

- perform a broad range of supervisory responsibilities
- produce written documents with clearly organized thought using proper English sentence construction, punctuation, and grammar
- communicate orally with customers, clients, and the public in face-to-face, one-on-one settings, in group settings, and using a telephone
- observe or monitor objects to determine compliance with prescribed operating or safety standards

- keep current on city fire codes and ordinances
- comprehend and make inferences from written materials such as fire codes and ordinances
- use graphic instructions such as blueprints, layouts, or other visual aids
- move light objects (under 20 pounds) short distances (20 feet or less)
- enter data or information into a terminal, PC, or other keyboard device
- work cooperatively with other city employees and the public
- work safely without presenting a direct threat to self or others.

Additional Requirements

- Some positions will require the performance of other essential and marginal functions, depending upon work location, assignment, or shift.
- Some positions require the use of personal or city vehicles on city business. Individuals must be physically capable of operating the vehicles safely, possess a valid driver's license, and have an acceptable driving record. Use of a personal vehicle for city business will be prohibited if the employee is not authorized by the city-designated physician to drive a city vehicle or if the employee does not have personal insurance coverage.
- One year of experience in fire protection engineering and a bachelor's degree in fire protection engineering or a related field is required. Other combinations of experience and education that meet the minimum requirements may be substituted for this requirement.

Companies Offering Fire Protection/Suppression Services

There are a growing number of companies that offer fire protection and/or suppression services to private and commercial sites, communities, wildlands, and airports. One example is Rural/Metro Corporation, which currently provides fire protection services to more than 25 communities and responds to more than 60,000 calls annually. To join its reserve program, from which firefighters are selected, applicants must

- ▶ be at least 21 years old
- ▶ possess a high school diploma or GED
- ▶ pass a physical agility test

▶ have an acceptable driving record

▶ pass a drug-screening test

▶ pass a written exam

Once applicants join the reserve program, they need to attend a fire academy on weekends and they can begin going on fire calls after completing a certain amount of training. While firefighters are members of the reserve program, they receive minimum wage for the fire calls they go on. Graduates from the academy are granted a Firefighter II certificate. For reserve firefighters who get hired as full-time career firefighters with Rural/Metro in Arizona, the starting annual salary is approximately $35,000. Contact Rural/Metro by calling 1-800-421-5718, or visit its website: www.ruralmetro.com.

Another such company is Wackenhut, which employs hundreds of full-time fire and EMS personnel. It provides fire protection, fire prevention, and emergency response services to commercial facilities such as the Kennedy Space Center, industrial facilities such as Saturn Corporation and Nissan Manufacturing Corporation, airports, and municipal locations that include towns, cities, and counties. Contact Wackenhut at its website: www.wackenhutservices.com.

Alpine Wildfire Services, located in Gardnerville, Nevada, provides emergency wildland fire suppression services as well as extended mop-up. Most of its staff are former federal firefighters, but it also trains employees through classes that meet the minimum National Wildfire Coordinating Group (NWCG) guidelines and regulations. Alpine Wildfire Services can be found at 1504 Highway 395 N, Unit 8, Suite 481, Gardnerville, NV 89410.

Other companies that hire out firefighter services are those that provide aerial firefighting. Below is a list of many of these employers, along with contact information.

Multiengine Air Tanker Companies

AERO FLITE, INC.

Matt Ziomek

4700 Flight Line Drive

Kingman, AZ 86401

520-757-1002

Fax 520-757-2951

E-mail: aerodc4@ctza.com

AERO UNION CORPORA-TION

Victor Alvistur (Assn President)

Charles Isele

100 Lockheed Avenue

Chico, CA 95973-9098

530-896-3000

Fax 350-893-8585

ALAMOGORDO MUNICIPAL AIRPORT

PO Box 340

Alamogordo, NM 88311

505-437-7360

Fax 505-434-6531

ARDCO, INC.

Gary Garrett

PO Box 23450

Tucson, AZ 85734-3450

520-883-4119

Fax 520-883-5858

E-mail: ARDCOINC@aol.com

BUTLER AIRCRAFT COMPANY

Dave Kelly

1050 SE Sisters Avenue

Redmond, OR 97756-8615

541-548-8166

Fax 541-548-0863

E-mail: ButlerAcft@aol.com

HAWKINS & POWERS AVIA-TION, INC.

Gene Powers

Duane Powers

PO Box 391

Greybull, WY 82426-0391

307-765-4482

Fax 307-765-2535

E-mail: handp@tctwest.net

HIRTH AIR TANKERS

Connie Hirth

160 Airport Road

Johnson County Airport

Buffalo, WY 82834-9357

307-684-7160

Fax 307-684-7160

INTERNATIONAL AIR RESPONSE

Woody Grantham

22000 South Price Road

Chandler, AZ 85248-1677

520-796-5188

Fax 520-796-1064

NEPTUNE, INC.

Mark Timmons

Kristen Schloemer

Missoula International Airport

5225 Highway 10 West, Box 17

Missoula, MT 59802-9318

406-542-0606

Fax 406-542-3222

T.B.M., INC.

Mr. Hank Moore

(Assn Treasurer)

243 Estate Street

Tulare, CA 93274-1932

559-686-3476

Fax 559-686-3477

Helitanker Companies

ERICKSON AIR-CRANE COMPANY

Kenneth Chapman

(F/F Manager)

PO Box 3247

Central Point, OR 97502-0010

541-664-5544

Fax 541-664-7613

HEAVY LIFT HELICOPTERS, INC.

Robin Rogers

PO Box 4

Clovis, CA 93613-0004

559-299-4903

Fax 559-292-5240

Single-Engine Air Tanker Companies

DOWNSTOWN AERO

Richard Nixholm

Curt Nixholm

Vern Baker

339 Harding Highway

Vineland, NJ 08360-9154

856-697-3300

Fax 856-697-2132

E-mail: FireCats1@aol.com

QUEEN BEE AIR SPECIAL-TIES, INC.

Chuck Kemper

PO Box 245

Rigby, ID 83442-0245

208-745-7654

Fax 208-745-6672

Sustaining Members

AIR TRACTOR, INC.

Leland Snow

PO Box 485

Olney, TX 76374-0485

940-564-5616

Fax 940-564-2348

ARNOLD KOLB

PO Box 1828

Alamogordo, NM 88310-1828

505-439-5621

Fax 505-437-8194

BIGHORN AIRWAYS, INC.

Robert Eisele

PO Box 4037

912 West Brundage Lane

Sheridan, Wyoming 82801

307-672-3421

Fax 307-674-4468

E-mail: bhairway@wavecom.net

PRECISION ENGINES

CORPORATION

Dave Cort

33220 100th Street SW, #E

Everett, Washington 98204

425-347-2800

Fax 425-353-9431

E-mail: dcort@pacpac.com

BYCAN-SELLEN

ASSOCIATES, INC.

Fred Talton

1800 Mallard Road

Smithfield, NC 27577

919-934-9896

Fax 919-934-9926

How to Apply

The biggest challenge in applying for jobs with private fire companies is to find out about job openings and the names of companies that are looking for firefighters. After you've tried contacting one or more of the companies listed above, try word of mouth. Ask any of the firefighters or fire instructors you know if they can give you possible leads on private fire company names and locations. You might want to consider subscribing to a firefighter recruitment service that includes private fire companies in its listings (see Appendix A for contact information).

Another way to find out about these jobs is to scour your local newspapers and phone books and ask your local public librarian for information about companies that appear to have a need for fire services, such as oil refineries or shipyards or companies in the chemical, aircraft and aerospace industries. Once you locate such companies, call their human resources department and inquire about possible openings.

JOB OPPORTUNITIES FOR THOSE LEAVING THE MILITARY

There are both direct and indirect benefits for people leaving the military who are seeking firefighting positions. An indirect benefit is that firefighter training and experience in the military is highly valued. Prospective employers may look more favorably on the applications of people who have been in the military, due to the high quality of firefighting training and experience those applicants received while serving in the military. The military's focus on the importance of teamwork and following orders is highly esteemed by many municipal fire chiefs. Members of the military who learn teamwork skills and who learn to follow a commander's orders while in the line of duty are considered well equipped to do the same in a fire department; therefore, if you have a military background, it is a plus for you.

A more direct benefit occurs for select groups of people who leave the military and, in some cases, their spouses. This direct benefit is normally referred to as veterans' preference. The preference may give job applicants extra points, ranging from 5 to 15, on a portion of the testing process. For example, if you meet the eligibility requirements, you could score a 100 on the written exam and be given an additional 5 points due to active military duty, which would result in a score of 105. Such a high score would most likely put you at or near the top of the eligibility list for most fire departments. Many military members who served in Operation Desert Storm are eligible for this direct benefit. Specific information about who qualifies for veterans' preference should be clearly spelled out in your job application. For more information on veterans' preference programs, you can call 912-757-3000 and select "Federal Employment Topics" and then "Veterans."

USING THE INTERNET TO HELP LAND THE JOB YOU WANT

The Internet has become a valuable resource for locating information about firefighting and for landing a job in this coveted field. We have already listed many websites for employers, ranging from small, private companies to the federal government. Aside from connecting with potential employers directly, there are other job search services you should be aware of.

Sites of interest to job seekers in the fire protection field include those of fire-related professional associations, bookstores, specific fire departments, recruitment agencies, and many others. Below are key fire-related websites that can help maximize your chances of landing the perfect job, from giving you general information on the different careers available to offering books for sale and bulletin boards to post questions on to giving you inside news from experienced firefighters across the country. You will find that many of these sites contain links to other sites that may also be of interest.

Professional Associations

Professional associations can give you general information about the fire service industry as well as specific information on a variety of topics within the field of fire protection. Check out the following websites for a variety of information, ranging from newsletters and fire statistics to educational resources and fire news.

www.nfpa.org

> This site contains the latest information about the National Fire Protection Association (NFPA), its departments, publications, seminars, and educational programs. The NFPA, which was organized in 1896, is the largest private organization devoted to fire protection. This site also has a good selection of links to other fire-related websites.

www.iaff.org

> This is the website for the International Association of Fire Fighters (IAFF). It offers legislative news, political actions, regulatory updates, a calendar of events, and other information of interest to firefighters.

www.usfa.fema.gov

> The U.S. Fire Administration (USFA) website offers a wealth of information about firefighting. The USFA was established by Congress in

1974; its mission is to provide leadership, coordination, and support for the nation's fire prevention and control, fire training and education, and emergency medical services activities. This website offers extensive free publications on a range of firefighting topics.

See the listing in Appendix B for more professional associations and other organizations of interest to firefighters.

Employment Recruitment Companies

These websites offer employment recruiting information for a fee to prospective firefighters and to firefighters looking for promotional opportunities. Review each company carefully before you commit to subscribing to a recruitment service. Each offers slightly different services and they all charge different fees. Recruitment companies can be especially helpful to prospective firefighters who are looking for openings in parts of the country other than where they live. Some of these sites also contain free fire-related information at their websites, such as bulletin boards, bookstores, links to other sites, and chat rooms.

www.firecareers.com

The Perfect Firefighter Candidate is a recruitment company that offers information about job openings, filing deadlines, salary, requirements, and who to contact or how to get involved in the testing process for each job listed. You can subscribe to a monthly e-mail notification service to get job information on all levels of jobs, from firefighter to fire chief. The website also offers a bulletin board, chat room, and books and other products for sale. New additions are scheduled to be added to this site.

www.psrjobs.com/fireems.htm

Public Safety Recruitment was established in 1993. It provides information from thousands of paid fire departments and EMS agencies across the nation. The monthly newsletter, weekly e-mail service, and 900 telephone numbers offer prospective applicants the names of recruiting agencies and detailed information about potential jobs, including contact information. Check its website for its latest fee schedule. It also offers an on-line bookstore where you can view descriptions of and order helpful firefighting books. You can e-mail your questions or comments to info@psrjobs.com.

www.IFPRA.com

This Website of IFPRA, the International Fire and Police Recruitment Administration, offers recruiting information to firefighter applicants.

See Appendix A for a more extensive list of fire service-specific employment resources.

Books, Videos, and Other Products

Here are some websites that offer fire-related books, videos, audiotapes, and other products of interest to firefighters and prospective firefighters:

www.firebooks.com

This site contains a firefighter's bookstore on-line. You can order a free catalog to see what books it offers or order directly from the site.

www.ifsta.org/catalog/prevention.html

A website for the International Fire Service Training Association (IFSTA) that offers a list of the 77 manuals it publishes.

www.fire-police-ems.com

This is the website for FSP Books and Videos, a company that sells books, videos, and other materials related to fire, police, and EMS. You can place orders directly from this site.

Wildland Firefighter Information

These sites offer information useful for prospective or active wildfire firefighters on the state or federal level:

www.nifc.gov

> The National Interagency Fire Center (NIFC), in Boise, Idaho, includes the nation's primary logistical support center for wildland fire suppression. Working with state and local agencies, NIFC provides national response to wildfires and other emergencies and serves as a focal point for wildland fire information and technology.

www.blm.gov:80/careers/employ5.html

> This Bureau of Land Management website discusses how to obtain federal firefighting jobs and offers a list of state agencies, including contact information.

www.neotecinc.com/wildfire

> This is the website of *Wildfire* magazine, which is published by the International Association of Wildland Fire. This magazine discusses wildland fire safety and current issues in wildland fire and is written by firefighters, fire managers, and experts in aviation and crew resource management.

Other Fire-Related Websites

Here are a variety of websites that contain information related to firefighting. You can look for job leads, keep up with industry changes, look for networking contacts, and stay abreast of fire-related news by accessing these sites on a regular basis.

www.rescue1.com/fire411.htm

> Rescue One offers a website containing information related to EMS, police, and fire occupations. It links you directly to the fire headquarters page, which contains a list of over 30 links to other fire-related websites, including specific fire departments across the nation, recruitment companies, federal and state government agencies, professional associations, and fire reports.

www.firefighting.com

This is an interactive website that offers news, press releases, and products. Current firefighters are invited to post information and news on the site.

www.firetv.com

This site offers press releases and news stories related to firefighting.

www.hotcity.com/911/911lk/newyork.shtml

This site has links to everything imaginable pertaining to 911, fire, police, and EMS. There are links to every police department in the United States, every fire department in the United States, Missing Children, EMS units, the Red Cross, Red Crescent, and many others.

Appendix C contains dozens of additional resources related to firefighting careers.

Job Links

www.fs.fed.us/fire/links2.shtml#employment

The U.S. Forest Service website is excellent and contains job links, fire news, maps, descriptions of firefighter jobs, and qualifications for jobs.

www.wildfiretrainingnet.com/links/cat27.shtml

Free wildfire job links, bookstore, vendors, library make this website a great resource for wildland firefighters.

www1.firejobs.com/ndes

The National Directory of Emergency Services website contains job listings, career tips, and links to fire service-related sites of interest.

THE INSIDE TRACK

Thomas J. Kichemaster II
Volunteer: Lieutenant/EMT/Fire Investigator
Philomath Rural Fire Protection District #4
Philomath, Oregon

I have been a volunteer firefighter/EMT for 16 years, 11 with the Philomath RFPD. I actually fell into it by accident. When I was 17 years old, I happened to be the first person to find a small grass fire that was quickly growing, and I decided to do something about it. I had someone call 911 and then I got a shovel and started to "line" the fire. The fire department showed up, I talked to them for a few minutes and found out they were a volunteer department and were looking for some people, and the rest is history.

I like to help people, and that is the best part of being a firefighter. I love to educate the public on ways to make themselves and loved ones safer, and I spend most of my time on these fire prevention activities. Public education has taught people just how dangerous fire is, and since I have been a volunteer I have seen less and less fires. The worst part of being a firefighter is the death and destruction I see.

As an investigator, my main duty is determining how and why a fire started—this includes interviewing witnesses, examining the fire scene, and managing scene safety and reports. I also have responsibility for the crews under my command on a call, and I'm the president of the district's volunteers.

Being a volunteer, I am on call 24 hours a day, seven days a week—I carry my pager with me all the time. Of course if I am at work or on vacation, I don't respond. Most paid departments, however, work what is called a 24/48—24 hours on and then 48 hours off. This is a great shift to work, since every workday is a Friday.

I would advise someone who wants to begin a career as a firefighter to get a degree in fire science and also to get paramedic certification. And remember that the learning never stops—the day you think you know it all is the day you will injure yourself or someone else.

CHAPTER three

BECOMING A CANDIDATE: EDUCATION

THIS CHAPTER describes the different types of fire-related training programs available. You'll see sample courses and get information on training programs across the country. You'll also learn why it may work to your advantage to go to college and earn a degree, even if it's not directly related to firefighting.

THE GROWING need for increased education in order to land a firefighting job cannot be ignored. While the published minimum requirements listed for getting a job as a career firefighter are often a high school diploma or its equivalent, the reality is that the vast majority of successful firefighter applicants possess significantly more education than that. Many applicants have earned a fire science certificate or associate's degree and several have also obtained EMT training and certification in order to successfully land a job in this highly competitive field.

All the firefighters interviewed for this book confirm that the trend in fire departments around the country is to require education beyond a high school diploma. A college degree sets an applicant above many of his or her peers, allows a firefighter to earn a higher salary than non-degree colleagues, and can be beneficial in the future. Many departments offer incentive pay for education. You can earn substantially more per year if you have a certain level of education. For instance, the Orlando, Florida, fire department pays $110 per month above base salary if you have a bachelor's degree. In Dallas, the amount rises to $120 per month. In addition, it is common practice to promote those with a college education first. Furthermore, once a firefighter retires, whether because of working a set number of years or because of an injury, a degree can translate into more employment options.

Even volunteer firefighters are facing stricter educational demands. Many states now require that volunteers meet the National Fire Protection Association's Standard 1001: Firefighter Professional Qualifications. To meet this standard, one must go through a rigorous basic training course that includes classroom and practical instruction.

Your local fire department can tell you the type of training job applicants have, as opposed to what is required, in your area. Ask if firefighter and/or EMT certification are needed to be hired as a municipal firefighter in your state. For example, in Florida, all job applicants must obtain Firefighter I and EMT certification before they can be hired by a municipal fire department.

There are several different routes to getting the fire-fighting training you need to compete successfully for a paid position. Below are descriptions of the major types of training programs available for all ages and experience levels, ranging from high school to bachelor's degrees.

HIGH SCHOOL PREPARATION

If you haven't yet completed high school, you can take courses that will help you to prepare for a career as a firefighter. College-prep courses will cover most of the essential material. Basic skills, such as reading comprehension, writing, computer literacy, and mathematics and science, must be learned and reinforced. To go even further with your training, take as many of the following classes as possible:

chemistry
biology
health

auto mechanics

carpentry

drafting

blueprint reading

technical drawing

building construction

physical education (PE)

computer training

Spanish or other languages

By building a strong educational foundation while still in high school, you'll increase your chances of succeeding in the next phase of your training, whether it's a certificate, a college degree, or an on-the-job training program.

JUST THE FACTS

In 1963 Fred Conway, chief of a volunteer fire department, invented a sticker, designed to fit the cradle of a phone, that put phone numbers for fire, police, and ambulance at everyone's fingertips. His company, Discount Labels, now prints millions of these phone stickers every year.

FIRE EXPLORER AND FIRE CADET PROGRAMS

Depending on your age, you may be able to join a Fire Explorer or a fire cadet program to get valuable firefighter training and experience. Both of these programs are offered in many locations throughout the country. Most of them are for people between the ages of 15 and 24. However, age requirements vary; some cadet programs accept applicants through age 35.

Fire Explorer Program

The Boy Scouts of America, through its subsidiary Learning for Life, sponsors Fire Explorer programs in many locations nationwide. Through this program, Explorers between the ages of 15 and 21 can learn about every aspect of fire fighting by working with an affiliated fire department. In many cases, Explorers are allowed to respond to calls and ride along as observers. While Explorers are trained in fire suppression, they are not allowed to go into a burning building. Supervised Explorers perform numerous tasks on which firefighters inside the building rely.

For a listing of Fire Explorer programs throughout the country, log on to www.firehouse.com/links/Organizations/Fire_Explorers. You can also get information about the Fire Explorer program by contacting the Boy Scouts of America, Fire Exploring Program, 1325 West Walnut Hill Lane, PO Box 152079, Irving, TX, 75015–2079, or by contacting your local fire department to see if it has a Fire Explorer program you are eligible for. Here's a list of requirements for becoming an Explorer:

▶ be a citizen or live within 10 miles of the city limits
▶ be between the ages of 14 and 21
▶ have no felony charges
▶ maintain a C average in school
▶ maintain a good standing in the community
▶ have a reliable source of transportation

Fire Cadet Programs

Many municipal fire departments offer cadet programs. These programs vary among departments, but most offer training to interested people between the ages of 18 and 35; some programs take cadets as young as 16, while others consider only applicants 21 or younger. Contact local fire departments to find out if they sponsor cadet programs and to inquire about eligibility requirements. Below are listed a number of different programs, which illustrate the range offered by individual fire departments.

High School Cadets
Some fire departments offer cadet firefighter programs for high school students. These programs are designed for 16 to 18 year olds who wish to receive training and participate in departmental activities. Cadet members

are required to have their guardian's permission to join and must maintain good academic standing in high school. Members are eligible for all training, but cannot ride "in charge" until they turn 18 years old. Some fire departments recruit high school seniors under a high school work-study program. If you are still in high school, ask your guidance counselor for additional information about fire cadet programs offered through your local fire departments. You can also search the Internet using key words such as "cadet firefighter" or "fire cadet program" along with your city or state.

One example of a high school cadet program is the Baltimore City Fire Department Cadet Program, which is offered to high school juniors and seniors attending Baltimore City public schools. It begins during the summer between the junior and senior year. The summer course includes driver's education for those who do not already have a license, as well as eight weeks of firefighter training. Cadets also receive EMT and physical fitness training.

During the following school year, cadets continue their training every afternoon after attending high school classes in the morning. In addition to class work, cadets spend time in fire departments, ambulance companies, and hospital emergency rooms. They go on relevant field trips and perform community service projects. Once a cadet graduates from high school, he or she may go on to college or be employed by the fire department. For more information, write to the Baltimore City Office of Employment Development, 101 West 24th Street, Baltimore, MD 21218.

College Student Cadets

One fire cadet program offered to college students is found in New York City. The FDNY Fire Safety Cadet Corps is a one-year program offered to students enrolled in a college or university within New York City. The Corps' goal is to establish a diverse pool of highly motivated students who train as firefighters, serve in the New York City fire department, and get the opportunity to take the New York City firefighters test as a promotional exam (those who pass are appointed ahead of all other applicants on the eligibility list).

The cadets spend several months participating in a rigorous course of study, working closely with a team of assigned mentors. Training includes courses in fire safety education, basic firefighting procedures, basic fire investigations, certified responder training, health and nutrition instruction, and physical fitness training. They also receive a wage of $8.60 per hour part-time (60 hours per month) during the school year and full-time during the summer. Additional benefits include a $4,000 student loan that is forgiven after two years' service as a firefighter.

To qualify for the cadet program, applicants must be:

▶ between 19 and 26 years of age
▶ a U.S. citizen or legal resident alien eligible for citizenship when appointed as a firefighter
▶ a resident of New York City
▶ enrolled in a college or university within New York City with a minimum of 18 credits and a 2.5 GPA (grade point average) or two years' full-time military service

To get more information about the FDNY Fire Safety Cadet Corps, write to them at 9 MetroTech, Brooklyn, NY 11201, or call 718-999-FDNY.

General Cadet Programs

As we've stated above, joining a fire cadet program is a good way to gain knowledge about a fire department, learn the basic skills of a firefighter, and get support, encouragement, and insight into pursuing a career in the fire service. Cadet programs are not limited to students. Many fire departments offer hands-on emergency medical training, work experience at fire stations, and training in firefighter skills for any cadets enrolled in their program. Eligible age levels vary among programs. As an example, the Phoenix, Arizona, fire department cadet program is described below.

Phoenix Cadet Program

Cadets receive hands-on emergency medical training, work experience at fire stations, training in firefighter skills, and volunteerism for the community. They are required to volunteer a minimum of 24 hours every three months to the fire department. This may be done in a variety of areas such as teaching CPR and helping with fire station open houses, public education events, or the service van program. Cadets are responsible for staffing the service van, which provides customer service support such as nonemergency transport for behavioral health incidents. Once on-duty, cadets notify the battalion chiefs to be placed on the roll call. Field battalion chiefs and captains supervise the on-duty staff of cadets.

To be eligible for the fire cadet program, you must

- be between 18 and 24 years of age
- be an EMT or be able to achieve certification within six months
- complete an application
- go through a selection board interview
- get a background check
- have a valid driver's license and a good driving record

CERTIFICATE PROGRAMS

There are different types of certificates, awarded upon the completion of specific training programs, that will help increase your chances of landing a great job. For example, many technical schools, community colleges, and other schools offer certificate programs in fire science or fire technology. You can also seek EMT certification, CPR training, or other first-aid training. Some fire departments now require that all new firefighters have EMT certification prior to being hired. Check with the fire departments to which you're considering applying to in order to find out about their specific requirements, as requirements often differ. If you need to obtain EMT certification, take a look at the book entitled *EMT Career Starter, Second Edition*, published by LearningExpress, to get the latest information about EMT requirements and to see an extensive directory of schools offering EMT training throughout the country.

Read all certificate materials carefully before you apply to any program of study. You should also speak to an instructor or guidance counselor at the school(s) you are considering, in order to find out if the fire science certificate offered is a good match for you. There may be several different certificates offered by one school that fall under the general heading of fire science, so you need to examine each certificate program carefully before enrolling. For example, some programs emphasize fire administration or fire inspection rather than firefighting. Other programs may be geared to people who are already employed as firefighters but need to obtain additional certification for a promotion or to master specialized skills.

Most certificate programs require that applicants have a high school diploma or its equivalent before beginning the certificate program. It is typical for programs to require regular attendance and an academic average of a C or higher to be eligible to receive a certificate upon completion of the course. Entrance requirements may include a physical ability exam and a medical exam. A one-year fire science administration certificate training program is detailed below. This program is offered at a college in Virginia. State residents pay $1,341.30, while nonresidents pay $5,825.33.

Fire Science Administration Certificate

Course Name	1st Semester	2nd Semester
College Composition I	3	
Introduction to Fire Science	3	
Hazardous Materials Response	3	
Introduction to Mathematics (or higher-level math course)	3	
Social science elective (economics, geography, history, political science, psychology, or sociology)	3	
Elective	1	
Fire Suppression Operations		3
Fire Prevention Fundamentals		3
Building Construction		3
Emergency Service Supervision		3
Introduction to Microcomputer Software		3
Introduction to Speech Communication		3
Total Credits Per Semester	16	18

In contrast to the Virginia program, a certificate course offered by a community college in Pennsylvania requires just one semester of study. It is designed for those pursuing a firefighting career as well as for those already employed in the field. The course costs $1,126 for a resident, $3,717 for a nonresident.

Fire Science Certificate

Course Name	Number of Credit Hours
Fire Protection Systems	3
Fire Investigation	3
Fire-Fighting Strategies and Tactics	3
Building Construction for the Fire Service	3
BOCA (Building Officials Code Administration)	
FirePrevention and Building Codes	3
Total Credits	**15**

Associate Degree Programs

An associate degree program's length of study is generally either two academic or two calendar years. Entrance requirements include a high school diploma (possibly with a college-prep course of study) or a GED. Many associate degree programs also require entrance and placement exams. An associate degree program differs from a certificate program in that some courses are taken in liberal arts along with the courses that are required for your major. Courses in your major combine classroom theory with practical application of the skills you need.

There are two types of schools that offer associate degree programs: community colleges and junior colleges. If you plan to live at home and work while getting your education, you might consider a community college. Community colleges are public institutions offering vocational and academic courses both during the day and at night. They typically cost less than both two- and four-year public and private institutions. Depending on your course of study, you could have one of the following when you are finished:

▶ an AA degree (associate in arts)
▶ an AS degree (associate in science)
▶ an AAS degree (associate in applied science)

You can find out the location of community colleges in your area by contacting your state's department of education. Or check the Internet through a search engine such as Yahoo.com for community colleges, which are listed by state.

Junior colleges are typically more expensive than community colleges, because they tend to be privately owned. You can earn a two-year degree (AA or AS), which can usually be applied to four-year programs at most colleges and universities. Use the Internet or the best-selling guide *Peterson's Two-Year Colleges 2001* to help you with your search.

Read all college materials carefully before you apply to an associate degree program. You should also speak to an instructor or guidance counselor at the school you are considering, in order to find out if the fire science associate's degree it offers is a good match for you. There may be several different specialties offered by one school that fall under the general heading of fire science, so you need to examine each associate degree program carefully before enrolling. For example, some degree programs emphasize fire administration or fire protection engineering rather than firefighting. Other programs are designed for people who are already employed as firefighters and are seeking additional training to prepare for a promotion or otherwise further their career.

Some associate degree programs combine both pre-employment students and post-employment students in the same class, so you could be studying alongside several career firefighters in one or more of your courses. If that's the case, take the opportunity to get to know them and ask questions so you'll be better prepared when you enter the job-hunting phase. A community college guidance counselor from Georgia says:

> Our associate degree program is made up of both career firefighters and people who want to become career firefighters. The courses are designed so each of these two groups can benefit from them. While our program is geared more for fire lieutenants and other firefighters, we always have a number of aspiring firefighters who enroll and who benefit from the courses.

An associate degree training program from a community college is listed below, to give you an idea of what you can expect. This is an evening program that leads to an associate in science degree in Fire Protection and Safety Technology. The total number of credit hours needed to complete the degree is 62.

Associate in Science Degree in Fire Protection and Safety Technology

Course	Credit Hours
English Composition	3
Introduction to Literature	3
Introduction to Fire Protection	3
Fundamentals of Fire Prevention	3
Hazardous Materials	3
Chemistry for Fire Service or Introduction to Chemistry	4
Fire Science Hydraulics	3
Fire Protection Systems and Equipment	3
Building Construction for the Fire Service	3
Law and the Fire Service	3
Mathematics elective	3
Humanities elective	3
Fire science electives (2)	6
Science elective	4
Introduction to Psychology	3
Introduction to Sociology	3
Social science elective	3
Electives (2)	6
Total Credits	**62**

A two-year college in New Jersey offers an associate's degree in Applied Science: Fire Science Technology. It is designed for those who will seek employment as municipal public safety officers, arson investigators, industrial safety inspectors, and fire insurance and fire suppression systems salespersons, as well as firefighters. In addition to classroom instruction, this course offers the opportunity for students to develop skills in using the most advanced fire science technology.

Associate in Applied Science Degree in Fire Science Technology

Course	Credit Hours
Composition I	3
Introduction to Fire Protection	3
College Mathematics	3
Introduction to Physical Science	3
Social science elective	3
Composition II or Speech Fundamentals	3
Fundamentals of Fire Prevention	3
Fire Science course	3
Social science elective	3
Humanities electives (2)	6
Hazardous Materials I	3
Fire Protection, Building Construction	3
Fire science courses (5)	15
Free electives (2)	6
Total Credits:	**60**

Bachelor Degree Programs

Colleges and universities offer undergraduate (four-year) programs in which you can earn a bachelor's degree (BA) and often a master's (MA) and a doctoral (PhD) degree in a variety of fields. Entrance requirements are more stringent than for community colleges; admissions personnel will expect you to have taken certain classes in high school to meet their admission standards. Your high school GPA and standardized test scores (most often those of the Scholastic Aptitude Tests, or SATs) will be considered. If your high school grades are weak or it has been some time since you were last in school, you might want to consider taking courses at a community college to bring you up to speed. You can always apply to the college or university as a transfer student after your academic track record has improved.

Be aware that state or public colleges and universities are generally less expensive to attend than private colleges and universities, because they receive state funds to offset its operational costs. Another thing to consider when choosing a college is their placement program in fire science. Does it have a relationship with area fire departments in which the departments actively recruit on campus and may even use the campus as the site for their training courses? Attending a school with such a relationship could greatly improve your chances of employment upon graduation.

Although many entry-level firefighters don't have a bachelor's degree, if you plan to advance in your career to the level of fire chief or want to become a fire protection engineer instead of a firefighter, a four-year degree is necessary. Below are listed some examples of courses leading to a bachelor's degree in Fire Protection Engineering. The list does not include all the courses required for a bachelor's degree, but will give you an idea of what to expect. These courses are offered at a major university in Maryland where annual tuition is $4,460 for state residents and $10,589 for nonresidents.

Fire Protection Engineer

Linear Algebra	Calculus
Differential Equations	General Physics I and II
Fire Dynamics	Mechanics of Materials
Introduction to Fire Protection Engineering	Fire Alarm and Special Hazards Design
Computer Applications	Fire Protection Fluid Mechanics
Fire Protection Systems Design I	Heat Transfer Applications in Fire Protection
Pyrometrics of Materials	Mechanics of Deformable Solids
Thermodynamics	Principles of Electrical Engineering
Fire Protection Hazard Analysis	Life Safety and Risk Analysis

Fire Academies

While many states have state-sponsored or private fire academies to train new municipal firefighters, these academies are normally for employed firefighters only. However, if a fire academy is affiliated with a community college, then prospective firefighters are normally able to enter the program. Requirements vary among states, so check carefully for fire academy entrance requirements.

IN THE NEWS

The Miami Fire-Rescue Training Center's minimum curriculum now takes 800 hours, or six months, to complete. Courses are given in areas such as firefighter standards, fire-fighting skills, rope rescue operations, basic water rescue, special ladders and skill drills, EMS orientation, state EMT training, and paramedic training. Once training is completed, firefighters face another five to six months of probation, during which they receive additional training.

Distance Training Programs

A growing number of programs are available that are designed for students to earn a degree in fire science at home, while working full- or part-time. Unlike community colleges, which often hold classes in the evenings and on weekends to accommodate work schedules, with distance training you never attend classes. Several colleges and universities now have programs with names like Degrees at a Distance, Correspondence Courses, or Long-Distance Learning that allow you to study and take courses on your own.

Distance learning is also known as independent study. It focuses on the idea that adults, through their jobs, personal activities, and general life experience, have many of the tools necessary to be successful independent learners. These tools include organizational and time management skills, basic writing and communication skills, and motivation and initiative. Adults also tend to make serious commitments to their education.

If you already have some work and life experience behind you and believe you are a good candidate for independent study, this could be an excellent way to get the fire service education you need. Distance learning can also be a good option for working firefighters who wish to complete their bachelor's degrees. Search the Internet with terms such as "distance learning" for schools that offer these programs. From sites such as Yahoo, you can find search categories under the term "education" that can help you. Also check Appendix C for books about distance learning programs.

National Fire Academy's Degrees at a Distance Program

One distance learning option for prospective firefighters is the Degrees at a Distance Program (DDP) sponsored by the National Fire Academy. It is offered by a network of accredited four-year colleges and universities that serve seven regions around the country. Course offerings are at the college junior and senior level. Through the DDP, you can take individual courses for credit to upgrade your professional skills; earn a certificate from the National Fire Academy for successfully completing six courses; or complete the entire curriculum and turn a two-year associate's degree into a four-year bachelor's degree.

The DDP's course curriculum is designed to supplement each participating institution's requirements for a bachelor's degree. Like traditional college courses, these programs include reading assignments, written exercises, and exams. And just because students don't go to actual classes doesn't mean they don't have meaningful contact with qualified instructors. Most students have conferences with instructors by telephone, mail, and computer. As with traditional schooling, assignments are returned to students with detailed comments and suggestions. When it is time for exams, students travel to a central location to take them.

Learning the DDP Way

Courses offered through the Degrees at a Distance Program cover a full range of topics important to firefighters and other fire service professionals, from fire science to administration to prevention technology. Although the DDP curriculum is aimed at the junior and senior levels, its course listing below is representative of the types of classes you can sign up for in traditional (nonindependent study) college programs at different academic levels.

- Fire Dynamics
- Police and Legal Foundations of Fire Protection
- The Community and Fire Threat
- Applications of Fire Research
- Incendiary Fire Analysis and Investigation
- Fire Protection Structure and Systems Design
- Fire-related Human Behavior

■ Fire Prevention Organization and Management

■ Analytic Approaches to Public Fire Protection

■ Personnel Management for the Fire Service

■ Advanced Fire Administration

■ Disaster and Fire Defense Planning

■ Managerial Issues in Hazardous Materials

You can contact the program's sponsor, the National Fire Academy, at the following address: National Fire Academy, Higher Education Programs, 16825 South Seton Avenue, Emmitsburg, MD 21727. You can also e-mail queries to Ed.Kaplan@fema.gov. If you wish to get information directly from participating colleges and universities, consult the list below.

Degrees at a Distance Program Colleges and Universities

School	Contact	Region
Cincinnati, University of	University of Cincinnati College of Applied Science 2220 Victory Parkway Cincinnati, OH 45206 513-556-6583 Fax 513-556-4856	Florida, Georgia, Indiana, Michigan, Minnesota, North Dakota, Ohio, South Dakota, Wisconsin
Cogswell College	Cogswell College 1175 Bordeaux Sunnyvale, CA 94089-1299 800-264-7955 Fax 408-747-0764	Arizona, California, Nevada
Memphis, University of	University College University of Memphis Johnson Hall G-1 Memphis, TN 38152 901-678-2754 Fax 901-678-4913	Alabama, Arkansas, Kentucky, Louisiana, Mississippi, South Carolina,Tennessee

School	Contact	Region
Empire State College/SUNY	Fire Service Coordinator Empire State College/SUNY Center for Distance Learning 2 Union Avenue Saratoga Springs, NY 12866 518-587-2100, ext. 300 Fax 518-587-2100, ext. 357	Connecticut, Maine, Massachusetts, New Hampshire, New York, Pennsylvania, Rhode Island, Vermont
Maryland, University of	University College University of Maryland Fire Science Undergraduate Programs Distance Education University Boulevard at Adelphi Road College Park, MD 20742 800-283-6832 or 301-985-7788 Fax 301-985-4615	Delaware, District of Columbia, Maryland, New Jersey, North Carolina, Virginia, West Virginia
Western Illinois University	Western Illinois University Extended Learning 401 Memorial Hall Macomb, IL 61445 309-298-2496 Fax 309-298-2133	Illinois, Iowa, Kansas, Missouri, Nebraska, New Mexico, Oklahoma, Texas
Western Oregon University	Western Oregon University Division of Extended and Summer Studies Monmouth, OR 97361 800-451-5767 or 503-838-8483 Fax 503-838-8473	Alaska, Colorado, Hawaii, Idaho, Montana, Oregon, Utah, Washington, Wyoming

HOW TO CHOOSE THE TRAINING PROGRAM THAT'S BEST FOR YOU

Since there are so many training programs, it can be a challenge to find the one that's best for you. The first step is to find out what schools near you offer fire science training or other college courses that will help you land a career firefighter job. Check the directory in Appendix D to find a list of some of the schools that offer fire-related training programs nationwide. You can also use the tips located throughout this chapter to conduct searches on the Internet.

The next step is to contact the schools for more information. You should always confirm that they currently offer courses related to fire services. Ask to speak to a guidance counselor or to someone in the fire science or fire technology department to get detailed information about the fire science programs offered. Request a school catalog and whatever brochures are available about the school and its programs. Read these documents carefully when you receive them, to find out the required courses for your program, how much it will cost, and how long the program will last.

It is worth the time to visit the schools you are interested in and talk to a guidance counselor or admissions officer at each one. These counselors are trained to help you identify your needs and decide if their school will meet them. Follow these steps when preparing for a campus visit:

1. Contact the office of admissions to request an appointment to visit. Remember to ask for the name of the person making the appointment and that of the person you will be meeting with. Try to schedule a meeting with an instructor in the fire science program as well as a guidance counselor in the admissions or counseling department.
2. Bring a copy of your transcript or permanent record card if you are meeting with an admissions officer.
3. Prepare a list of honors or awards you received in high school or the community, including documentation of any volunteer or fire cadet training.
4. Ask to tour the fire science practical experience area, if possible. This tour will show you the available equipment and materials for simulations and other fire exercises. Many schools are affiliated with one or more local fire departments or private fire academies, so they offer this hands-on training through another agency.
5. Be prepared to ask questions about the school and the surrounding community, including extracurricular activities, work opportunities, and anything else you don't find explained in the promotional brochures.

Questions to Ask

After you visit several schools and narrow your choices down to two or three, you will need to ask tough questions about each program in order to make the final selection. You want to attend the school that will best serve your needs, help you land a job, and charge fees that you can afford (see Chapter 4 for information on securing financial aid). You may choose to apply to several programs if the admissions at your top-choice school are competitive. The following questions will assist you in determining which school is your top choice. After each question, you will find the information you need to hear for an answer.

1. Does the fire science or fire technology program admit students who are not currently full-time paid firefighters?

This is an important question to ask as a first step in evaluating a school's program. Years ago, most fire science degree programs were aimed at career firefighters who wanted to get promoted or move into a specialized area in the fire service. That has changed. Due to the competition for career fire-fighter positions, many more associate degree and certificate programs are available to help people gain the firefighting knowledge and experience that will set them above the crowd. Some schools advertise that they are geared to helping students learn all they can about firefighting and land a great job upon graduation. Other schools may allow only career firefighters who are working full-time at a local fire department into their program.

Depending on the requirements in your county or state, you may need to enroll in a certificate training program rather than an associate degree program in order to pass the state's examination and certification process. This is currently the standard procedure in Florida, for example. Schools also have different programs of study and different areas of specialization, such as fire protection engineering or technology, fire administration, firefighting, fire technology, and fire inspection, in addition to or under the heading of fire science.

Therefore you need to contact each school you are considering and ask to speak to an instructor or a representative of the fire science or fire technology program. Ask specifically if you can enroll in the school's fire science program with your background and credentials, and find out what type of students the school admits to each program, to see if a certificate or an associate degree program would be best for you. Even if you can't enroll in a program as a degree-seeking student, you may be able to take selected courses on an audit basis. It doesn't hurt to ask, and any fire-related courses that you take can only improve your chances of landing your first job.

2. What requirements must be met to attend?

Entrance requirements vary. You may be required to do any one or more of the following:

- ▶ take English, math, or science placement tests
- ▶ Take and achieve a certain score on the SATs or ACT (if you have not already taken them in high school)
- ▶ submit a certain GPA from high school
- ▶ take a physical exam
- ▶ take a physical ability test

If one of the schools you are considering has an entrance requirement you might not meet, call an admissions counselor to discuss your case. Many schools offer some type of remedial help if needed so students can meet the requirement in the future.

3. What are the qualifications of the faculty?

There should be some faculty members with bachelor's or master's degrees in fire science and/or faculty members who have extensive experience as firefighters and firefighter instructors. The faculty should be accessible to students for advisory meetings and conferences to discuss class work.

4. Is the school accredited?

It's important that the school you choose be accredited. Accreditation is a rigorous and complex process that ensures sound educational and ethical business practices at the schools that achieve it. It is a process schools undergo voluntarily.

Some accrediting agencies are national and some are regional. The name of the accrediting agency for the school you're interested in will probably be plainly printed on the school's general catalog, because schools are usually proud of their accredited status. If you can't locate the information in a school's printed materials, you can make sure of their status by calling the school and asking for the name(s) of its accrediting agency or agencies.

An important point to remember is that if the school you choose is not accredited, you cannot get financial aid through any government programs. (See Chapter 4 for more information about how to obtain financial aid.)

5. Does the school have access to the latest firefighting equipment and technology?

It's a good idea, when you are visiting schools to ask to see their fire service training equipment. Current firefighting technology and training should be available to students. The hands-on portion of the training program should cover basic firefighting principles and should offer simulation exercises to practice the basic skills needed by a firefighter, such as:

▶ Fire Hose Techniques
▶ Extinguishing fires in test modules
▶ How to move while wearing heavy equipment
▶ Working in smoke-filled rooms
▶ Pump operations
▶ Confined space rescue

6. How much will the program cost?

Tuition varies according to the length of the program, the area in which the school is located, and whether you are a resident of the state in which you are applying for school. If the tuition is not listed in the college's course catalog, call the school and ask what its current resident and nonresident rates (whichever applies to you) are. As you can see from the sample tuition costs listed above in the programs (certificate, associate, and bachelor's), there is quite a range of costs for completing a training program.

Don't forget to include the following items when figuring out how much each school will cost:

▶ books and supplies
▶ admission fees

- lab fees
- miscellaneous fees (parking, other mandatory fees such as student activity fees for full-time students at some schools regardless of program of study, and so on)
- room and board or rent
- transportation
- childcare (if required)
- loan origination fees (if applicable)
- personal expenses

After you create an estimate of the total costs for each school you are considering, you'll be armed with one more item that can make or break a school's desirability for you.

7. What is the student-teacher ratio?

The student-teacher ratio is a statistic that shows the average number of students assigned to one teacher in a classroom or lab. It's important that the student-teacher ratio not be too high. Education suffers if classrooms are too crowded or if a teacher has too many students to be able to see everyone who wishes to be seen for a private conference. According to one of the top national accrediting agencies, the Accrediting Council for Independent Colleges and Schools (ACICS), a reasonable student-teacher ratio for skills training is 30 students to 1 teacher in a lecture setting and 15 students to 1 teacher in a laboratory or clinical instruction setting. At very good schools the ratio is even better than the ACICS recommends.

8. When are classes scheduled?

If you need to work full- or part-time during regular business hours while attending school, you'll need to find a school that offers classes at nontraditional times, such as evenings or weekends.

9. Is the campus environment suitable?

When you visit the school, determine how the campus feels to you. Is it too big? Too small? Too quiet? Is the campus in a city or a rural community? Is it easily accessible? Do you need to rely on public transportation to get there? Select a school that has a campus environment that meets your needs.

10. Does the school offer child care facilities?

This may be of concern to you. If it is, you'll want to tour the child care facilities and interview the people who work there to see if the care is suitable for your children.

Application Tips from Admissions Directors

- Apply as early as you can. You'll need to fill out an application and submit high school or GED transcripts and any copies of SAT, ACT, or other test scores used for admission. If you haven't taken these tests, you may have to before you can be admitted. Call the school and find out when the next program starts, then apply at least a month or two before, to make sure you can complete requirements before the program begins.

- You may receive a prewritten request for high school transcripts from the admissions office when you get your application. Forward the request quickly, so the admissions process is not held up in any way.

- Make an appointment as soon as possible to take any placement tests that may be required.

- Pay your fees before the deadline. Enrollment is not complete each quarter or semester until students have paid all fees by the date specified on the registration form. If the fees are not paid by the deadline, their class registration may be canceled. If you are hoping to receive financial aid, apply as early as you can.

- Find out early in the application process if you must pass a physical or have any other medical history forms on file for the school you choose.

INSIDE TRACK

Ken Hendrix

Captain

Dallas Fire Department

My interest in the fire service derives from the fact that my father was in the department, and during my visits to the fire station one of the main things I noticed was the quality of the people—they all seemed like good guys, the kind of people you would want to be around. I have generally found this to be true over the course of my career. It was during my second year of college that I began to seriously look at the fire service as a career, and I was 22 years old when I became a member of the department. That was

24 years ago, and even back then there was so much competition that it took me two-and-a-half years to get hired. Nowadays many fire departments have a huge volume of applicants, sometimes in the hundreds, so it can take a lot of personal commitment to get the job you want.

The fire service is a tremendously challenging and rewarding career. There is nothing like the feeling you get from being able to put a good stop on a fire or being able to make a difference in someone's life in a time of crisis. One thing about the job that really keeps it interesting for me is that you never know what is going to happen next. Another benefit is that your advancement is largely determined by your own initiative, skills, and willingness to apply yourself. It is the type of career where a lot of what you get out of it depends on what you put into it. I enjoy the fact that I am in a career where even after 24 years I still look forward to going to work.

Our work schedule is 24 hours on duty and 48 hours off. There are routine daily activities at the station such as equipment readiness checks, inventory, station maintenance, and company training, among others. In addition we are involved in building inspections, hydrant maintenance, smoke detector installations, and other public service activities. The activities we are most often involved in are training, equipment readiness, and inspections.

The fire service has changed significantly over the years, especially in terms of the expansion of the scope of services we provide to the public. The fields of EMS, HAZMAT, and specialized rescue have become more prevalent in the fire service since I began my career. Recently the fire service has begun to take on more of the responsibility for responding to the threats posed by weapons of mass destruction, including chemical, biological and nuclear incidents.

For someone considering the fire service as a profession, my advice would be to learn as much as possible about the organization you are attempting to join and to understand the scope of the services they deliver. A lot of departments provide EMS service as well as fire suppression. The EMS aspect can be very challenging and is often the bulk of the service delivery, especially in those departments where firefighters serve as paramedics as well. EMS places its own set of physical and mental demands on an individual in addition to the rigors of performing the duties necessary to being an effective firefighter. Make sure you fully understand the responsibilities of the job and are prepared to make the commitment necessary to meet the challenges and demands that you will face.

CHAPTER four

BECOMING A CANDIDATE: FINANCIAL AID

THIS CHAPTER explains the three types of financial aid available: scholarships and grants, loans, and work-study programs. You'll find out how to determine your eligibility, which financial records you'll need to gather, and how to complete and file forms (a sample financial aid form is included). At the end of the chapter are listed many more resources that can help you find the aid you need.

YOU HAVE decided that you want a job in fire protection services, and you've chosen a training program. Now you need a plan for financing your training. Whether your goal is a certificate, associate's degree, or bachelor's degree, be assured that you can qualify for aid at several different types of schools, ranging from community colleges, technical colleges, and universities to vocational schools that offer short-term training programs. You can often qualify for some type of financial aid even if you're attending only part time. The financial aid you'll get may be less than in full-time programs, but it can still be worthwhile and help you pay for a portion of your fire services training.

Don't let financial aid anxiety deter you from exploring the many options you have for financing your training program. After you've read this chapter, investigate the other resources listed in it. The Internet is probably the best source for up-to-the-minute information, and almost all of it is free. If you are in school or have been accepted to a school already, take advantage of financial aid advisors, whose job is to address your concerns and help you fill out the necessary paperwork.

SOME MYTHS ABOUT FINANCIAL AID

The subject of financial aid is often misunderstood. Here are three of the most common myths.

Myth #1: *All the red tape involved in finding sources and applying for financial aid is too confusing for me.*

Fact: It's really not that confusing. The whole financial aid process is a set of steps that are ordered and logical. Besides, several sources of help are available. To start with, read this chapter carefully to get a helpful overview of the entire process and tips on how to get the most financial aid possible. Then use one or more of the resources listed within and at the end of this chapter for additional help. If you believe you'll be able to cope with college, you'll be able to cope with looking for the money to finance your education, especially if you take the process one step at a time in an organized manner.

Myth #2: *For most students, financial aid just means getting a loan and going into heavy debt, which isn't worth it, or working while in school, which will lead to burnout and poor grades.*

Fact: Both the federal government and individual schools award grants and scholarships, which the student doesn't have to pay back. It is also possible to get a combination of scholarships and loans. It's worth taking out a loan if it means attending the school you really want to attend, rather than set-tling for your second choice or not going to school at all. As for working, it's true that it is a challenge to hold down a full-time or even part-time job while in school. However, a small amount of work-study employment (10–12 hours per week) has been shown to actually improve academic per-formance, because it teaches students important time-management skills.

Myth #3: *I can't understand the financial aid process because of all the unfamiliar terms and strange acronyms that are used.*

Fact: While you will encounter an amazing number of acronyms and some unfamiliar terms when applying for federal financial aid, you can refer to the acronym list and the glossary at the end of this chapter for quick definitions and clear explanations of the commonly used terms and acronyms.

TYPES OF FINANCIAL AID

There are three categories of financial aid:

1. Grants and scholarships—aid that you don't have to pay back
2. Work-study—aid that you earn by working
3. Loans—aid that you have to pay back

Grants

Grants are normally awarded based on financial need. Below are the two most common grants.

Federal Pell Grants

Federal Pell Grants are based on financial need and are awarded only to undergraduate students who have not yet earned a bachelor's or professional degree. For many students, Pell Grants provide a foundation of financial aid to which other aid may be added. For the year 1999–2000, the maximum award was $3,125. You can receive only one Pell Grant in an award year, and you may not receive Pell Grant funds for more than one school at a time.

How much you get will depend not only on your expected family contribution (EFC) but also on your cost of attendance, whether you're a full-time or a part-time student, and whether you attend school for a full academic year or less. You can qualify for a Pell Grant even if you are enrolled only part-time in a training program. You should also be aware that some private and school-based sources of financial aid will not consider your eligibility if you haven't first applied for a Pell Grant.

Federal Supplemental Educational Opportunity Grants (FSEOGs)

FSEOGs are for undergraduates with exceptional financial need, that is, students with the lowest EFCs. Priority is given to students who receive Pell Grants. An FSEOG is similar to a Pell Grant in that it doesn't need to be paid back.

You can receive between $100 and $4,000 a year, depending on when you apply, your level of need, and the funding level of the school you're attending. There's no guarantee that every eligible student will be able to receive a FSEOG. Students at each school are paid based on the availability of funds at that school, and not all schools participate in this program. To have the best chances of getting this grant, apply as early as you can after January 1 of the year in which you plan to attend school.

Scholarships

Scholarships are almost always awarded for academic merit or for special characteristics (for example, ethnic heritage, interests, sports, parents' careers, college major, and geographic location) rather than financial need. As with grants, you do not pay back your award money. Scholarships may be offered from federal, state, school, and private sources.

The best way to find scholarship money is to use one of the free search tools available on the Internet. After entering the appropriate information about yourself, a search takes place that ends with a list of those prizes for which you are eligible. Try www.fastasp.org, which bills itself as the world's largest and oldest private-sector scholarship database. Other good sites for conducting searches are www.collegescholarships.com and www.gripvision.com. If you don't have easy access to the Internet or want to expand your search, your high school guidance counselors or college financial aid officers also have plenty of information about available scholarship money.

To find private sources of aid, spend a few hours in the library looking at scholarship and fellowship books or consider a reasonably priced (under $30) scholarship search service. Use caution when dealing with scholarship search services. While most are perfectly legitimate, some scams have been reported. If you're unsure, contact a financial aid officer. See the resources section at the end of this chapter to find contact information for search services and scholarship book titles. Another place to check is in fire service magazines. If you're currently employed, find out if your employer has funds available for education. If you're a dependent student, ask your parents and other relatives to check with groups or organizations they belong to for possible aid sources. Consider these popular sources of scholarship money:

- ► religious organizations
- ► fraternal organizations
- ► clubs, such as Rotary, Kiwanis, American Legion, or 4H
- ► athletic clubs
- ► veterans groups
- ► ethnic group associations
- ► unions

If you already know which school you will attend, check with a financial aid administrator (FAA) in the financial aid department to find out if you qualify for any institutional scholarships or other aid. Many schools offer merit-based aid for students with a high school GPA of a certain level or with a certain level of SAT scores, in order to attract more students to their school. The National Merit Scholarship Corporation awards 5,000 students annually a scholarship based solely on outstanding academic performance. Check with the fire science department to see if it maintains a bulletin board or other method of posting available scholarships specific to fire science programs.

While you are looking for sources of scholarships, continue to enhance your chances of winning one by participating in extracurricular events and volunteer activities. You should also obtain references from people who know you well and are leaders in the community, so you can submit their names and/or letters with your scholarship applications. Make a list of any awards you've received in the past or other honors that you could list on your scholarship application.

There are thousands of scholarships awarded to students planning to enter the fire community. Below are samples. More information about these scholarships may be found at www.umuc.edu/studserv/finaid.html. To find more sources, search the Internet with terms such as "firefighting" and "scholarship."

Yvorra Leadership Development Scholarship Foundation

The Yvorra Leadership Development Foundation offers scholarships to members of emergency service organizations. These include volunteer, part-paid, and career personnel from fire departments, rescue squads, and emergency medical services. Contact the foundation at PO Box 408, Port Republic, MD 20676, or call 410-586-3048 for more information.

International Association of Arson Investigators (IAAI)

The IAAI offers scholarships of $1,000 for undergraduate students enrolled in fire science programs at two- and four-year institutions. The student must be a member of IAAI or sponsored by a member. Write to The John Charles Wilson Scholarship Fund at 300 South Broadway, Suite #100, St. Louis, MO 63102.

Maryland State Scholarship Administration

Maryland residents who are pursuing a degree in firefighting or other safety majors at a Maryland school and who agree to serve in Maryland as firefighters or rescue squad members for a certain amount of time after graduation may be eligible for a scholarship from the Maryland State Higher Education Commission. Contact the Maryland State Higher Education Commission, 16 Francis Street, Annapolis, MD 21401, for more information.

Texas Higher Education Coordinating Board

Applicants must be firefighters enrolled in a fire science degree program. The scholarship award is an exemption from tuition at public colleges or universities in Texas. Contact the Texas Higher Education Coordinating Board, PO Box 12788, Austin, TX 78711, for more information.

A program that benefits mainly middle-class students is the Hope Scholarship Credit. Eligible taxpayers may claim a credit for tuition and fees up to a maximum of $1,500 per student (the amount is scheduled to be reindexed for inflation after 2001). The credit applies only to the first two years of postsecondary education, and students must be enrolled at least half-time. Families whose adjusted gross income is $80,000 or more are ineligible. To find out more about the Hope Scholarship credit, log on to www.sfas.com.

Work-Study Programs

When applying to a college or university, you can indicate that you are interested in a work-study program. You'll then be given details about the types of jobs offered in various programs—which range from giving tours of the campus to prospective students to working in the cafeteria, or shelving library books—and how much they pay.

There is also the possibility of getting money for college by first securing a job with a fire department that agrees to cover all or part of your educational expenses. Many departments offer a tuition reimbursement program, which pays for all or part of your education. Some departments will pay only for classes related to your job. What qualifies as a job-related course may be defined in a detailed formal policy or you may have to get your classes approved on a case-by-case basis. Fire departments that offer this benefit include those in Columbus, Ohio; Detroit, Michigan; Fort Worth, Texas; Memphis, Tennesse; and Miami and Orlando, Florida.

Some departments make it even easier to attend college by permitting supervisors to adjust your work shifts and schedules so that you can attend classes. Others offer financial incentives not only for college classes, but also for advanced state certification courses and certain in-service training programs.

You may also want to investigate the Federal Work-Study (FWS) program, which can be applied for on the Free Application for Federal Student Aid, or FAFSA. The FWS program provides jobs for undergraduate and graduate students with financial need, allowing them to earn money to help pay education expenses. It encourages community service work and provides hands-on experience related to your course of study when available. The amount of the FWS award depends on

▶ when you apply (again, apply early)
▶ your level of need
▶ the funds available at your particular school

FWS salaries are the current federal minimum wage or higher, depending on the type of work and skills required. As an undergraduate, you'll be paid by the hour (a graduate student may receive a salary), and you will receive the money directly from your school; you cannot be paid by commission or fee. The awards are not transferable from year to year, and you will need to check with the schools to which you're applying to find out if the program is available; not all schools have work-study programs in every area of study.

An advantage of working under the FWS program is that your earnings are exempt from FICA (Federal Insurance Contribution Act) taxes if you are enrolled full-time and are working less than half time. You will be assigned a job on campus, in a private nonprofit organization, or with a public agency that offers a public service. You might provide a community service relating to fire or other emergency service if your school has such a program. Some schools have agreements with private for-profit companies whose work demands fire or other emergency skills. The total hourly wages you earn in each year cannot exceed your total FWS award for that academic year and you cannot work more than 20 hours per week. Your financial aid administrator or the direct employer must consider your class schedule and your academic progress before assigning you a job.

IN THE NEWS

In the year 2000, the International Association of Fire Fighters (IAFF) was the largest national sponsor of the Muscular Dystrophy Association. Firefighters raised a total pledge of 14 million dollars through such fund-raisers as marathons, car washes, and the "Firefighters Fill the Boot" campaign.

Student Loans

Although scholarships and grants and even work-study programs can help offset the costs of higher education, they usually don't give you enough money to pay your way entirely. Most students who can't afford to pay for their entire education rely at least in part on student loans. The largest single source of these loans—and for all money for students—is the federal government. Try these three sites for information about the U.S. government's educational funding programs:

www.fedmoney.org

This site explains everything from the application process (you can actually download the applications you'll need) and eligibility requirements to the different types of loans available.

www.finaid.org

Here you can find a calculator for figuring out how much money your education will cost (and how much you'll need to borrow), get instructions for filling out the necessary forms, and even find information on the various types of military aid available (which will be detailed in the next chapter).

www.ed.gov/offices/OSFAP/Students

This is the federal student financial aid home page. The FAFSA can be filled out and submitted online.

You can also get excellent detailed information about different sources of federal education funding by sending away for a copy of the U.S. Department of Education's publication *The Student Guide*. Write to the Federal Student Aid Information Center, PO Box 84, Washington, DC 20044, or call 800-4FED-AID.

Below are listed some of the most popular federal loan programs.

Federal Perkins Loans

A Perkins loan has the lowest interest (currently 5%) of any loan available for both undergraduate and graduate students and is offered to students with exceptional financial need. You repay your school, which lends the money to you with government funds.

Depending on when you apply, your level of need, and the funding level of the school, you can borrow up to $4,000 for each year of undergraduate study. The total amount you can borrow as an undergraduate is $20,000.

The school pays you directly by check or credits your tuition account. You have nine months after you graduate (provided you were continuously enrolled at least half-time) to begin repayment, with up to 10 years to pay off the entire loan.

Federal PLUS Loans (Parent Loans for Undergraduate Students)

PLUS loans enable parents with good credit histories to borrow money to pay the educational expenses of a child who is a dependent undergraduate student enrolled at least half-time. Your parents must submit the completed forms to your school.

To be eligible, your parents will be required to pass a credit check. If they don't pass, they might still be able to receive a loan if they can show that extenuating circumstances exist or if someone who is able to pass the credit check agrees to co-sign the loan. Your parents must also meet citizenship requirements.

The yearly limit on a PLUS Loan is equal to your cost of attendance minus any other financial aid you receive. For instance, if your cost of attendance is $6,000 and you receive $4,000 in other financial aid, your parents could borrow up to, but no more than, $2,000. The interest rate varies, but is not to exceed 9% over the life of the loan. Your parents must begin repayment while you're still in school. There is no grace period.

Federal Stafford Loans

Stafford Loans are low-interest loans that are given to students who attend school at least half-time and meet other eligibility requirements. The maximum amount you can borrow is $23,000 as a dependent undergraduate student. The lender is either the U.S. Department of Education or a bank you select, depending on the loan program under which you borrow. Check with your financial aid office for details. Stafford Loans fall into one of two categories:

▶ **Subsidized loans**, awarded on the basis of financial need
You will not be charged any interest on these loans before you begin repayment or during authorized periods of deferment. The federal government "subsidizes" the interest during these periods.
▶ **Unsubsidized loans**, not awarded on the basis of financial need
You'll be charged interest on an unsubsidized loan from the time it is disbursed until it is paid in full. If you allow the interest to accumulate, it will be capitalized; that is, the interest will be added to the principal amount of your loan, and additional interest will be based upon the higher amount. This will increase the amount you have to repay.

There are many borrowing limit categories to these loans, depending on whether you get an unsubsidized or a subsidized loan, which year in school you're enrolled for, how long your program of study is, and whether you're considered independent or dependent for purposes of federal aid eligibility. You can have both kinds of Stafford Loans at the same time, but the total amount of money loaned at any given time cannot exceed $23,000 for dependent students and $46,000 for independent students. The interest rate varies, but should not exceed 8.25%. An origination fee for a Stafford Loan is approximately 3% or 4% of the loan, and the fee will be deducted from each loan disbursement you receive. There is a six-month grace period after graduation before you must start repaying the loan.

Loan money is also available from state governments. Below is a list of the agencies responsible for giving out such loans, with websites and e-mail addresses where available.

ALABAMA

Alabama Commission on Higher Education

100 North Union Street

PO Box 302000

Montgomery, AL 36130-2000

334-242-2276

ALASKA

Alaska Commission on Postsecondary

Education

3030 Vintage Boulevard

Juneau, AK 99801-7109

907-465-6741

Fax 907-465-5316

ARIZONA

Arizona Commission for Postsecondary

Education

2020 North Central Avenue, Suite 275

Phoenix, AZ 85004-4503

602-229-2591

Fax 602-229-2599

Website: www.acpe.asu.edu

ARKANSAS

Arkansas Department of Education

4 State Capitol Mall, Room 107A

Little Rock, AR 72201-1071

501-682-4396

E-mail: finaid@adhe.arknet.edu

CALIFORNIA

California Student Aid Commission

PO Box 419026

Rancho Cordova, CA 95741-9026

916-526-7590 (Customer Service

Department)

Fax 916-323-2619

COLORADO

Colorado Commission on Higher Education

Colorado Heritage Center

1300 Broadway, Second Floor

Denver, CO 80203

303-866-2723

Fax 303-860-9750

CONNECTICUT

Connecticut Department of Higher
Education
61 Woodland Street
Hartford, CT 06105-2326
860-947-1855
Fax 860-947-1311

DELAWARE

Delaware Higher Education Commission
Carvel State Office Building, Fourth Floor
820 North French Street
Wilmington, DE 19801
302-577-3240
Fax 302-577-6765

DISTRICT OF COLUMBIA

Department of Human Services
Office of Postsecondary Education
Research and Assistance
2100 Martin Luther King Jr. Avenue SE,
Suite 401
Washington, DC 20020
202-727-3688
Fax 202-727-2739

FLORIDA

Florida Department of Education
Office of Student Financial Assistance
1344 Florida Education Center
325 West Gaines Street
Tallahassee, FL 32399-0400
888-827-2004
Fax 850-488-3612

GEORGIA

Georgia Student Finance Commission
2082 East Exchange Place, Suite 100
Tucker, GA 30084
770-724-9030
Website: www.gsfc.org

HAWAII

Hawaii State Postsecondary Education
Commission
2444 Dole Street, Room 209
Honolulu, HI 96822-2394
808-956-8207
Fax 808-956-5156

IDAHO

Idaho State Board of Education
PO Box 83720
Boise, ID 83720-0037
208-334-2270
Fax 208-334-2632

ILLINOIS

Illinois Student Assistance Commission (ISAC)
1755 Lake Cook Road
Deerfield, IL 60015-5209
800-899-4722
Website: www.isac-online.org

INDIANA

State Student Assistance Commission of
Indiana
150 West Market Street, Suite 500
Indianapolis, IN 46204-2811
317-232-2350
Fax 317-232-3260

IOWA

Iowa College Student Aid Commission

200 10th Street, Fourth Floor

Des Moines, IA 50309-3609

515-281-3501

E-mail: csac@max.state.ia.us

Website: www.iowacollegeaid.org

KANSAS

Kansas Board of Regents

700 SW Harrison, Suite 1410

Topeka, KS 66603-3760

785-296-3517

Fax 785-296-0983

E-mail: christy@kbor.state.ks.us

Website: www.ukans.edu/~kbor

KENTUCKY

Kentucky Higher Education Assistance

Authority (KHEAA)

1050 U.S. 127 South

Frankfort, KY 40601-4323

800-928-8926

Fax 502-696-7345

E-mail: webmaster@kheaa.com

Website: www.kheaa.com

LOUISIANA

Louisiana Office of Student Financial

Assistance

PO Box 91202

Baton Rouge, LA 70821-9202

800-259-5626 ext 1012

-or-

225-922-1012

Fax 225-922-1089

E-mail (for students):

custserv@osfa.state.la.us

-or-

webmaster@osfa.state.la.us

Website: www.osfa.state.la.us

MAINE

Finance Authority of Maine

PO Box 949

Augusta, ME 04332-0949

800-228-3734

-or-

207-623-3263

TDD: 207-626-2717

Fax 207-626-8208

E-mail: info@famemaine.com

MARYLAND

Maryland Higher Education Commission

Jeffrey Building, 16 Francis Street

Annapolis, MD 21401-1781

410-974-5370

Fax 410-974-5994

MASSACHUSETTS

Massachusetts Board of Higher Education

Office of Student Financial Assistance

330 Stuart Street, Third Floor

Boston, MA 02116

617-727-1205

Fax 617-727-0667

MICHIGAN

Michigan Higher Education Assistance
Authority
Office of Scholarships and Grants
PO Box 30462
Lansing, MI 48909-7962
517-373-3394
Fax 517-335-5984

MINNESOTA

Minnesota Higher Education Services Office
1450 Energy Park Drive, Suite 350
St. Paul, MN 55108-5227
800-657-3866
-or-
651-642-0567
Website: www.mheso.state.mn.us

MISSISSIPPI

Mississippi Postsecondary Education
Financial Assistance Board
3825 Ridgewood Road
Jackson, MS 39211-6453
601-982-6663
Fax 601-982-6527

MISSOURI

Missouri Student Assistance Resource
Services (MOSTARS)
3515 Amazonas Drive
Jefferson City, MO 65109-5717
800-473-6757
-or-
573-751-3940
Fax 573-751-6635

Website: www.mocbhe.gov/mostars/
finmenu.htm

MONTANA

Office of Commissioner of Higher Education
Montana Guaranteed Student Loan Program
PO Box 203101
Helena, MT 59620-3101
800-537-7508
E-mail: scholars@mgslp.state.mt.us
Website: www.mgslp.state.mt.us

NEBRASKA

Coordinating Commission for Postsecondary
Education
PO Box 95005
Lincoln, NE 68509-5005
402-471-2847
Fax 402-471-2886
Website: www.nol.org/nepostsecondaryed

NEVADA

Nevada Department of Education
700 East Fifth Street
Carson City, NV 89701-5096
775-687-9200
Fax 775-687-9101

NEW HAMPSHIRE

Postsecondary Education Commission
2 Industrial Park Drive
Concord, NH 03301-8512
603-271-2555
Fax 603-271-2696
E-mail: jknapp@nhsa.state.nh.us
Website: www.state.nh.us

NEW JERSEY

Higher Education Student Assistance
Authority
PO Box 540
Trenton, NJ 08625
800-792-8670
Fax 609-588-3316
Website: www.state.nj.us/treasury/osa

NEW MEXICO

New Mexico Commission on Higher
Education
1068 Cerrillos Road
Santa Fe, NM 87501
800-279-9777
E-mail: highered@che.state.nm.us
Website: www.nmche.org

NEW YORK

New York State Higher Education Services
Corporation
One Commerce Plaza
Albany, NY 12255
888-697-4372
Fax 518-473-3749

NORTH CAROLINA

North Carolina State Education Assistance
Authority
PO Box 13663
Research Triangle Park, NC 27709-3663
800-700-1775
E-mail: information@ncseaa.edu

NORTH DAKOTA

North Dakota University System
North Dakota Student Financial Assistance
Program
600 East Boulevard Avenue, Dept. 215
Bismarck, ND 58505-0230
701-328-4114
Fax 701-328-2961

OHIO

Ohio Board of Regents
PO Box 182452
Columbus, OH 43218-2452
888-833-1133
Fax 614-752-5903

OKLAHOMA

Oklahoma State Regents for Higher Education
500 Education Building
Oklahoma City, OK 73105-4503
405-858-4356
Fax 405-858-4577

OREGON

Oregon State Scholarship Commission
1500 Valley River Drive, Suite 100
Eugene, OR 97401-2130
800-452-8807
Fax 541-687-7419
Website: www.ossc.state.or.us

PENNSYLVANIA

Pennsylvania Higher Education Assistance
Authority
1200 North Seventh Street
Harrisburg, PA 17102-1444
800-692-7435
Website: www.pheaa.org

RHODE ISLAND

Rhode Island Higher Education Assistance
Authority
560 Jefferson Boulevard
Warwick, RI 02886
401-736-1170
Fax 401-736-3541
TDD: 401-222-6195

SOUTH CAROLINA

South Carolina Higher Education Tuition
Grants Commission
PO Box 12159
Columbia, SC 29211
803-734-1200
Fax 803-734-1426
Website: www.state.sc.us/tuitiongrants

SOUTH DAKOTA

Department of Education and Cultural Affairs
Office of the Secretary
700 Governors Drive
Pierre, SD 57501-2291
605-773-3134
Fax 605-773-6139

TENNESSEE

Tennessee Student Assistance Corporation
404 James Robertson Parkway, Suite 1950
Nashville, TN 37243
800-342-1663
615-741-1346
Fax 615-741-6101
Website: www.state.tn.us/tsac

TEXAS

Texas Higher Education Coordinating Board
PO Box 12788, Capitol Station
Austin, TX 78711
800-242-3062
Fax 512-427-6420

UTAH

Utah State Board of Regents
Utah System of Higher Education
355 West North Temple
#3 Triad Center, Suite 550
Salt Lake City, UT 84180-1205
801-321-7200
Fax 801-321-7299

VERMONT

Vermont Student Assistance Corporation
PO Box 2000
Winooski, VT 05404-2601
800-642-3177
-or-
800-655-9602
Fax 800-654-3765
E-mail: info@vsac.org
Website: www.vsac.org

VIRGINIA

State Council of Higher Education for
Virginia
James Monroe Building
101 North Fourteenth Street
Richmond, VA 23219-3684
804-786-1690
Fax 804-225-2604

WASHINGTON

Washington State Higher Education
Coordinating Board
PO Box 43430
917 Lakeridge Way
Olympia, WA 98501-3430
360-753-7850
Fax 360-753-7808
E-mail: info@hecb.wa.gov
Website: www.hecb.wa.gov

WEST VIRGINIA

State College and University Systems of
West Virginia Central Office
1018 Kanawha Boulevard East, Suite 700
Charleston, WV 25301-2827
304-558-4016
Fax 304-558-0259

WISCONSIN

Higher Educational Aids Board
PO Box 7885
Madison, WI 53707-7885
608-267-2944
Fax 608-267-2808
Website: http://heab.state.wi.us

WYOMING

Wyoming Community College Commission
2020 Carey Avenue, Eighth Floor
Cheyenne, WY 82002
307-777-7763
Fax 307-777-6567

Questions to Ask before You Take Out a Loan

In order to get the facts regarding the loan you're about to take out, ask the following questions:

1. *What is the interest rate and how often is the interest capitalized?* Your college's financial aid administrator will be able to tell you this.

2. *What fees will be charged?* Government loans generally have an origination fee, which goes to the federal government or the bank, depending on the loan program, to help offset its costs, and a guarantee fee, which goes to a guaranty agency for insuring the loan. Both are deducted from the amount given to you.

3. *Will I have to make any payments while still in school?* Usually you won't and, depending on the type of loan, the government may even pay the interest for you while you're in school.

4. *What is the grace period, the period after my schooling ends, during which no payment is required? Is the grace period long enough, realistically, for me to find a job and get on my feet?* A six-month grace period is common.

5. *When will my first payment be due, and approximately how much will it be?* You can get a good preview of the repayment process from the answer to this question.

6. *Who exactly will hold my loan? To whom will I be sending payments? Whom should I contact with questions or inform of changes in my situation?* Your loan may be sold by the original lender to a secondary market institution, in which case you will be notified as to the contact information for your new lender.

7. *Will I have the right to prepay the loan, without penalty, at any time?* Some loan programs allow prepayment with no penalty but others do not.

8. *Will deferments and forbearances be possible if I am temporarily unable to make payments?* You need to find out how to apply for a deferment or forbearance if you need it.

9. *Will the loan be canceled ("forgiven") if I become totally and permanently disabled or if I die?* This is always a good option to have on any loan you take out.

APPLYING FOR FINANCIAL AID

Now that you're aware of the types of aid available, you'll want to begin applying as soon as possible. You've heard about the FAFSA many times in this chapter already and have an idea of its importance. This is the form used by federal and state governments, as well as school and private funding sources, to determine your eligibility for grants, scholarships, and loans. The easiest way to get a copy is to log onto www.ed.gov/offices/OSFAP/students, where you can also find help in completing the form; you can then submit the completed form electronically. You can also get a copy by calling 800-4-FED-AID or stopping by your public library or your school's financial aid office. Be sure to get an original form, because photocopies of federal forms are not accepted.

The second step of the process is to create a financial aid calendar. Using any standard calendar, write in all of the application deadlines for each step of the financial aid process. You will be able to see at a glance what needs to be done when. Start this calendar by writing in the date you requested your FAFSA. Then mark down when you received it and when you sent in the completed form. Add important dates and deadlines for any other applications you need to complete for school-based or private aid as you progress though the financial aid process. Using and maintaining a calendar will help the whole financial aid process run more smoothly and give you peace of mind that the important dates are not forgotten.

JUST THE FACTS

Smoke jumpers wear approximately 80 pounds of equipment when they jump from a plane, including a padded Kevlar jumpsuit and helmet with a metal face grate. Each pair of jumpers gets a "fire box," which is dropped by parachute and contains tools, food, and water to support them for up to 48 hours.

When to Apply

Apply for financial aid as soon as possible after January 1 of the year in which you want to enroll in school. For example, if you want to begin school in the fall of 2001, then you should apply for financial aid as soon as possible after January 1, 2001. It is easier to complete the FAFSA after you have completed your tax return, so you may want to consider filing your taxes as early as possible as well. You *can* complete the FAFSA with estimated information and correct it after taxes are filed, so don't use incomplete tax returns as an excuse not to do the FAFSA early—it only hurts your chances of receiving maximum aid. Do not sign, date, or send your application before January 1 of the year for which you are seeking aid. If you apply by mail, send your completed application in the envelope that came with the original application. The envelope is already addressed, and using it insures that your application reaches the correct address. Do not send the FAFSA by FedEx, UPS, or other overnight mail, as it will not get there (the FAFSA is sent to a post office box). You can apply over the Web; contact the Department of Education on-line (see p. 121) for details.

Many students lose out on thousands of dollars in grants and loans because they file their applications too late. A financial aid administrator from New Jersey says:

When you fill out the Free Application for Federal Student Aid (FAFSA), you are applying for all aid available, both federal and state, work-study, student loans, et cetera. The important thing is complying with the deadline date. Those students who do are considered for the Pell Grant, the SEOG (Supplemental Educational Opportunity Grant), and the Perkins Loan, which is the best loan as far as interest goes. Lots of students miss the June 30th deadline, and it can mean losing $2,480 from TAG, about $350 from WPCNJ, and another $1,100 from EOF. Students, usually the ones who need the money most, often ignore the deadlines.

After you mail in your completed FAFSA, your application will be processed in approximately four weeks. Then you will receive a Student Aid Report (SAR) in the mail. The SAR will disclose your expected family contribution (EFC), the number used to determine your eligibility for federal student aid. Each school you list on the application may also receive your application information if the school is set up to receive it electronically.

You must reapply for financial aid every year. However, after your first year, you will receive an SAR in the mail before the application deadline. If no corrections need to be made, you can just sign it and send it in.

Getting Your Forms Filed

Follow these three simple steps if you are not completing and submitting the FAFSA online:

1. Get an original Federal Application for Federal Student Aid (FAFSA). Remember to pick up an original copy of this form, as photocopies are not acceptable.
2. Fill out the entire FAFSA as completely as possible. Make an appointment with a financial aid counselor if you need help. Read the form completely, and don't skip any relevant portions.
3. Return the FAFSA before the deadline date. Financial aid counselors warn that many students don't file the forms before the deadline and thus lose out on available aid. Don't be one of those students!

Financial Need

Financial aid from many of the programs discussed in this chapter is awarded on the basis of need (the exceptions include unsubsidized Stafford, PLUS, and consolidation loans, and some scholarships and grants). When you apply for federal student aid by completing the FAFSA, the information you report is used in a formula established by the U.S. Congress. The formula determines your EFC, the amount you and your family are expected to contribute toward your education. If your EFC is below a certain amount, you'll be eligible for a Pell Grant, assuming you meet all other eligibility requirements.

There is no maximum EFC that defines eligibility for the other financial aid options. Instead, your EFC is used in an equation to determine your financial needs.

Cost of Attendance — EFC = Financial Need

A financial aid administrator calculates your cost of attendance and subtracts the amount you and your family are expected to contribute toward that cost. If there's anything left over, you're considered to have financial need.

Are You Considered Dependent or Independent?

Federal policy uses strict and specific criteria to determine whether a student is dependent or independent and those criteria apply to all applicants for federal student aid equally. A dependent student is expected to have a parental contribution to school expenses, and an independent student is not. The parental contribution depends on the number of parents with earned income, their total income and assets, the age of the older parent, the family size, and the number of family members enrolled in postsecondary schools. Income is not just the adjusted gross income from the tax return, but also includes nontaxable income such as social security benefits and child support.

You're an independent student if *at least one* of the following applies to you:

▶ you are 24 years of age (for the academic year 2000–01, you must have been born before January 1, 1977; for 2000–01, you must have been born before January 1, 1978)
▶ you are married (even if you are separated)
▶ you have legal dependents other than a spouse who get more than half of their support from you and will continue to get that support during the award year
▶ you are an orphan or ward of the court (or were a ward of the court until age 18)
▶ you are a graduate or professional student
▶ you are a veteran of the U.S. Armed Forces, formerly engaged in active service in the U.S. Army, Navy, Air Force, Marines, or Coast Guard or as a cadet or midshipman at one of the service academies and released under a condition other than dishonorable discharge. (ROTC students, members of the National Guard, and most reservists are not considered veterans, nor are cadets and midshipmen still enrolled in one of the military service academies.)

▶ you have special and unusual circumstances that can be documented to your college financial aid administrators (for example, abuse in the family, alcoholism, and so on). This is extremely rare, and only an experienced financial aid administrator at your college can make this "dependency override" on the FAFSA application. Denial of an override request cannot be appealed to the Department of Education. The financial aid administrator's decision is final.

If you live with your parents and if they claimed you as a dependent on their last tax return, then your need will be based on your parents' income. You do not qualify for independent status just because your parents have decided not to claim you as an exemption on their tax return (this used to be the case but is no longer) or do not want to provide financial support for your college education.

Students are classified as dependent or independent because federal student aid programs are based on the idea that students (and their parents or spouse, if applicable) have the primary responsibility for paying for their postsecondary education.

Gathering Financial Records

Your financial need for most grants and loans depends on your financial situation. Once you've determined whether you are considered a dependent or an independent student, you'll know whose financial records you need to gather for this step of the process. If you are a dependent student, then you must gather not only your own financial records, but also those of your parents, because you must report their income and assets as well as your own when you complete the FAFSA. If you are an independent student, then you need to gather only your own financial records (and those of your spouse if you're married). Gather your tax records from the year prior to the one in which you are applying. For example, if you are applying for financial aid for the fall of 2001, you will use your tax records from the year 2000.

To help you fill out the FAFSA, gather the following documents:

- U.S. income tax returns (IRS Form 1040, 1040A, or 1040EZ) for the year that just ended and W-2 and 1099 forms
- records of untaxed income, such as social security benefits, AFDC (Aid to Families with Dependent Children) or ADC (Aid to Dependent Children) payments, child support, welfare, pensions, military subsistence allowances, and veteran's benefits
- current bank statements and mortgage information
- medical and dental expenses for the past year that weren't covered by health insurance
- business and/or farm records
- records of investments, such as stocks, bonds, and mutual funds, as well as bank certificates of deposit (CDs) and recent statements from money market accounts
- social security number(s)

Even if you do not complete your federal income tax return until March or April, you should not wait to file your FAFSA until your tax returns are filed with the IRS. Instead, use estimated income information and submit the FAFSA, as noted earlier, just as soon as possible after January 1. Be as accurate as possible, knowing that you can correct estimates later.

GENERAL GUIDELINES FOR LOANS

Before you commit yourself to any loans, be sure to keep in mind that they will need to be repaid. Estimate realistically how much you'll earn when you leave school, remembering that you'll have other monthly obligations such as housing, food, and transportation expenses.

Once You're in School

Once you have your loan(s) and you're attending classes, you should start to take responsibility for it. Keep a file of information on your loan that includes copies of all your loan documents and related correspondence, along with a record of all your payments. Open and read all your mail about your education loan.

Remember also that you are obligated by law to notify both your financial aid administrator and the holder or servicer of your loan if there is a change in your:

▶ name
▶ address
▶ enrollment status (dropping to less than half-time means that you'll have to begin payment six months later)
▶ anticipated graduation date

After You Leave School

After graduation, you must begin repaying your student loan immediately or after a stated grace period. For example, if you have a Stafford Loan, you will be provided with a six-month grace period before your first payment is due; other types of loans have grace periods as well. If you haven't been out in the world of work before, you'll begin your credit history with your loan repayment. If you make payments on time, you'll build up a good credit rating, and credit will be easier for you to obtain for other things. Get off to a good start, so you don't run the risk of going into default. If you default or refuse to pay back your loan, any number of the following things could happen to you as a result. You could:

▶ have trouble getting any kind of credit in the future
▶ no longer qualify for federal or state educational financial aid
▶ have holds placed on your college records
▶ have your wages garnished
▶ have future federal income tax refunds withheld
▶ have your assets seized

You should also remember that your financial status might be examined as part of your background check when applying to a fire department. A bad credit history could prevent you from achieving your goal of becoming a firefighter. To avoid the negative consequences of going into default in your loan, be sure to do the following:

- ▶ Open and read all mail you receive about your education loans immediately.
- ▶ Make scheduled payments on time; since interest is calculated daily, delays can be costly.
- ▶ Contact your loan servicer immediately if you can't make payments on time; he or she may be able to get you into a graduated or income-sensitive/income-contingent repayment plan or work with you to arrange a deferment or forbearance.

There are a few circumstances under which you won't have to repay your loan. If you become permanently and totally disabled, you probably will not have to (providing the disability did not exist prior to your obtaining the aid). Likewise, if you die, if your school closes permanently in the middle of the term, or if you are erroneously certified for aid by the financial aid office, you will not have to make payments on the loan. However, if you're simply disappointed in your program of study or don't get the job you wanted after graduation, you are not relieved of your obligation.

Loan Repayment

When it comes time to repay your loan, you will make payments to your original lender, to a secondary market institution to which your lender has sold your loan, or to a loan servicing specialist acting as its agent to collect payments. At the beginning of the process, try to choose the lender that offers you the best benefits (for example, a lender that lets you pay electronically, offers lower interest rates to those who consistently pay on time and/or has a toll-free number to call 24 hours a day, 7 days a week). Ask the financial aid administrator at your college to direct you to such lenders.

Be sure to check out your repayment options before borrowing. Lenders are required to offer repayment plans that will make it easier to pay back your loans. Your repayment options may include:

- ▶ **Standard repayment:** full principal and interest payments due each month throughout your loan term. You'll pay the least amount of interest using the standard repayment plan, but your monthly payments may seem high when you're just out of school.

- ▶ **Graduated repayment:** interest-only or partial interest monthly payments due early in repayment, with payment amounts increasing thereafter. Some lenders offer interest-only or partial interest repayment options that provide the lowest initial monthly payments available.

- ▶ **Income-based repayment:** monthly payments based on a percentage of your monthly income.

- ▶ **A consolidation loan:** several types of federal student loans with various repayment schedules consolidated into one loan. This loan is designed to help student or parent borrowers simplify their loan repayments. The interest rate on a consolidation loan may be lower than what you're currently paying on one or more of your loans. The phone number for loan consolidation at the William D. Ford Direct Loan Program is 800-557-7392. Financial administrators recommend that you do not consolidate a Perkins loan with any other loans, since the interest on a Perkins loan is already the lowest available. Loan consolidation is not available from all lenders.

- ▶ **Prepayment:** paying more than is required on your loan each month or in a lump sum. This option is allowed for all federally sponsored loans at any time during the life of the loan without penalty. Prepayment will reduce the total cost of your loan.

It's quite possible—in fact likely—that while you're still in school your FFELP (Federal Family Education Loan Program) loan will be sold to a secondary market institution such as Sallie Mae. You'll be notified of the sale by letter, and you need not worry if this happens; your loan terms and conditions will remain exactly the same, or they may even improve. Indeed, the sale may give you repayment options and benefits that you would not have had otherwise. Your payments after you finish school and your requests for information should be directed to the new loan holder.

If you receive any interest-bearing student loans, you will have to attend exit counseling after graduation, where the loan lenders will tell you the total amount of your debt and work out a payment schedule with you to determine the amounts and dates of repayment. Many loans do not become due until at least six to nine months after you graduate, giving you a grace period. For example, you do not have to begin paying on the Perkins loan until nine months after you graduate. This grace period is to give you time to find a good job and start earning money. However, during this time, you may have to pay the interest on your loan.

If for some reason you remain unemployed when your payments become due, you may receive an unemployment deferment for a certain length of time. For many loans, you will have a maximum repayment period of 10 years (excluding periods of deferment and forbearance).

THE MOST FREQUENTLY ASKED QUESTIONS ABOUT FINANCIAL AID

Here are answers to the most frequently asked questions about student financial aid:

1. *I probably don't qualify for aid. Should I apply for it anyway?* Yes. Many students and families mistakenly think they don't qualify for aid and so fail to apply. Remember that there are some sources of aid that are not based on need. The FAFSA form is free—there's no good reason for not applying.
2. *Do I need to be admitted at a particular university before I can apply for financial aid?* No. You can apply for financial aid any time after January 1. However, to get the funds, you must be admitted and enrolled in school.
3. *Do I have to reapply for financial aid every year?* Yes, and if your financial circumstances change, you may get either more or less aid. After your first year, you will receive a renewal application that contains preprinted information from the previous year's FAFSA. Renewal of your aid also depends on your making satisfactory progress toward a degree and achieving a minimum GPA.
4. *Are my parents responsible for my educational loans?* No. You and you alone are responsible for your loans, unless your parents endorse or co-sign them. Parents are, however, responsible for the federal PLUS loans. If your parents (or grandparents or uncle or distant cousins) want to help

pay off your loan, you can have your billing statements sent to their address.

5. *If I take a leave of absence from school, do I have to start repaying my loans?* Not immediately, but you will after the grace period. Generally, if you use your grace period up during your leave, you'll have to begin repayment immediately after graduation unless you apply for an extension of the grace period before it's used up.

6. *If I get assistance from another source, should I report it to the student financial aid office?* Yes—and, sadly, your aid amount will probably be lowered accordingly. But you'll get into trouble later on if you don't report it.

7. *Are federal work-study earnings taxable?* Yes, you must pay federal and state income tax on them, although you may be exempt from FICA taxes if you are enrolled full-time and work less than 20 hours a week.

8. *My parents are separated or divorced. Which parent is responsible for filling out the FAFSA?* If your parents are separated or divorced, the custodial parent is responsible for filling out the FAFSA. The custodial parent is the parent with whom you lived the most during the past 12 months. Note that this is not necessarily the same as the parent who has legal custody. The question of which parent must fill out the FAFSA becomes complicated in many situations, so you should take your particular circumstances to the student financial aid office for help.

Financial Aid Checklist

❏ Explore your options as soon as possible once you've decided to begin a training program.

❏ Find out what your school requires and what financial aid it offers.

❏ Complete and mail the FAFSA as soon as possible after January 1.

❏ Complete and mail other applications by their deadlines.

❏ Gather loan application information and forms from your college financial aid office.

❏ Complete the student (and parent, for PLUS Loans) portion of loan applications and submit to the school for processing. Don't forget to sign the loan application.

❏ Carefully read all letters and notices from the school, the federal student aid processor, the need analysis service, and private scholarship organizations. Note whether financial aid will be sent before or after you are notified about admission, and note exactly how you will receive the money.

❏ Return all documents the financial aid office asks for promptly.

❏ Report any changes in your financial resources or expenses to your financial aid office so your award can be adjusted accordingly.

❏ Reapply each year.

Financial Aid Acronyms Key

COA	Cost of Attendance
CWS	College Work-Study
EFC	Expected Family Contribution
EFT	Electronic Funds Transfer
ESAR	Electronic Student Aid Report
ETS	Educational Testing Service
FAA	Financial Aid Administrator
FAF	Financial Aid Form
FAFSA	Free Application for Federal Student Aid
FAO	Financial Aid Office
FDSLP	Federal Direct Student Loan Program
FFELP	Federal Family Education Loan Program
FSEOG	Federal Supplemental Educational Opportunity Grant
FWS	Federal Work-Study
GSL	Guaranteed Student Loan (now called subsidized Stafford Loan)
PC	Parent Contribution
PLUS	Parent Loan for Undergraduate Students
SAP	Satisfactory Academic Progress
SC	Student Contribution
SLS	Supplemental Loan for Students (now called unsubsidized Stafford Loan)
USED	U.S. Department of Education

FINANCIAL AID TERMS—CLEARLY DEFINED

Accrued interest: Interest that accumulates on the unpaid principal balance of your loan

Capitalization of interest: Addition of accrued interest to the principal balance of your loan that increases both your total debt and monthly payments

Default: Failure to repay your educational loan

Deferment: A period during which a borrower who meets certain criteria may suspend loan payments

Delinquency: Failure to make payments when due

Disbursement: Loan funds issued by the lender

Forbearance: Temporary adjustment to repayment schedule for cases of financial hardship

Grace period: The specified period of time after you graduate or leave school during which you need not make loan payments

Holder: The institution that currently owns your loan

In-school, grace, and deferment interest subsidy: Interest the federal government pays for borrowers on some loans while the borrower is in school, during authorized deferments, and during grace periods

Interest: The cost you pay to borrow money

Interest-only payment: A payment that covers only interest owed on tahe loan and none of the principal balance

Lender (Originator): The organization that puts up the money when you take out a loan; most lenders are financial institutions, but some state agencies and schools make loans too

Origination fee: A fee, deducted from the principal of a loan, that is paid to the federal government to offset the cost of the subsidy to borrowers under certain loan programs

Principal: The amount you borrow, which may increase as a result of capitalization of interest, and the amount on which you pay interest

Promissory note: A contract between you and the lender that includes all the terms and conditions under which you promise to repay your loan

Secondary markets: Institutions that buy student loans from originating lenders, thus providing lenders with funds to make new loans

Servicer: The organization that administers and collects your loan; the service may be the holder of your loan or an agent acting on its behalf

Subsidized Stafford Loans: Loans based on financial need; the government pays the interest on a subsidized Stafford Loan for borrowers while they are in school and during specified deferment periods

Unsubsidized Stafford Loans: Loans available to borrowers regardless of family income; unsubsidized Stafford Loan borrowers are responsible for the interest during in-school, deferment, and repayment periods

FINANCIAL AID RESOURCES

In addition to the sources listed throughout this chapter, these are additional resources that may be used to obtain more information about financial aid.

Telephone Numbers

Federal Student Aid Information Center
(U. S. Department of Education)

Hotline	800-4-FED-AID
	-or-
	800-433-3243
TDD for the hearing-impaired	800-730-8913
For suspicion of fraud or abuse of federal aid	800-MIS-USED (800-647-8733)
Selective Service	847-688-6888
Immigration and Naturalization (INS)	415-705-4205
Internal Revenue Service (IRS)	800-829-1040
Social Security Administration	800-772-1213
National Merit Scholarship Corporation	708-866-5100
Sallie Mae (college answer service)	800-222-7183
Career College Association	202-336-6828

American College Testing (ACT)	
(for information about forms	
submitted to the need analysis servicer)	916-361-0656
College Scholarship Service (CSS)	609-771-7725
TDD	609-883-7051
Need Access/Need Analysis Service	800-282-1550
FAFSA on the WEB (for processing/software problems)	800-801-0576

Websites

www.ed.gov/prog_info/SFAStudentGuide

The Student Guide is a free informative brochure about financial aid and is available on-line at the Department of Education's website listed here.

www.ed.gov\prog_info\SFA\FAFSA

This site offers students help in completing the FAFSA.

www.ed.gov/offices/OPE/t4_codes.html

This site offers a list of Title IV school codes that you may need to complete the FAFSA.

www.ed.gov/offices/OPE/express.html

This site enables you to fill out and submit the FAFSA on-line. You'll need to print out, sign, and send in the release and signature pages.

www.career.org

This is the website of the Career College Association (CCA), which offers a limited number of scholarships for attendance at private proprietary schools. You can also contact the CCA at 750 First Street NE, Suite 900, Washington, DC 20002–4242.

www.salliemae.com

The Sallie Mae website contains information about loan programs.

Software Programs

Cash for Class
800-205-9581
Fax 714-673-9039

Chronicle Guidance Publications
PO Box 1190
Moravia, NY 13118-1190
C-LECT Financial Aid Module
800-622-7284
-or-
315-497-0330
Fax 315-497-3359

Peterson's Award Search
PO Box 2123
Princeton, NJ 08543-2123
800-338-3282
-or-
609-243-9111
E-mail: custsvc@petersons.com

Pinnacle Peak Solutions (Scholarships 101)
7735 East Windrose Drive
Scottsdale, AZ 85260
800-762-7101
-or-
602-951-9377
Fax 602-948-7603

Redheads Software, Inc.
3334 East Coast Highway, #216
Corona del Mar, CA 92625
E-mail: cashclass@aol.com

TP Software (Student Financial Aid Search Software)
PO Box 532
Bonita, CA 91908-0532
800-791-7791
-or-
619-496-8673
E-mail: mail@tpsoftware.com

Books and Pamphlets

Cassidy, Daniel J. *The Scholarship Book 2000: The Complete Guide to Private-Sector Scholarships, Fellowships, Grants, and Loans for the Undergraduate.* Englewood Cliffs, NJ: Prentice Hall, 1999.

Chany, Kalman A. and Geoff Martz. *Student Advantage Guide to Paying for College* 1997 ed. New York: Random House, The Princeton Review, 1997.

College School Service. *College Costs & Financial Aid Handbook.* 18th edition. New York: The College Entrance Examination Board, 1998.

Cook, Melissa L. *College Student's Handbook to Financial Assistance and Planning.* Traverse City, MI: Moonbeam Publications, Inc., 1991.

Davis, Kristen. *Financing College: How to Use Savings, Financial Aid, Scholarships, and Loans to Afford the School of Your Choice.* Washington, DC: Random House, 1996.

Hern, Davis and Joyce Lain Kennedy. *College Financial Aid for Dummies.* New York: IDG Books Worldwide, 1999.

How Can I Receive Financial Aid for College? Published from the Parent Brochures ACCESS ERIC Website. Order a printed copy by calling 800-LET-ERIC or write to ACCESS ERIC, Research Boulevard, MS 5F, Rockville, MD 20850-3172.

Peterson's Guides. *Peterson's Scholarships, Grants and Prizes 2000.* Princeton, NJ: Peterson's, 1999.

———. *Scholarships, Grants & Prizes: Guide to College Financial Aid from Private Sources.* Princeton, NJ: Peterson's, 1998.

Ragins, Marianne. *Winning Scholarships for College: An Insider's Guide.* New York: Henry Holt & Co., 1994.

Schlacter, Gail and R. David Weber. *Scholarships 2000*. New York: Kaplan, 1999.

Schwartz, John. *College Scholarships and Financial Aid*. New York: Simon & Schuster, Macmillan, 1995.

U.S. Department of Education. *Looking for Student Aid*. Washington, DC: U.S. Department of Education, [annual]. To get a printed copy of this overview of sources of information about financial aid, call 800-4-FED-AID.

————. *The Student Guide*. Washington, DC: U.S. Department of Education, [annual]. To get a printed copy of this handbook about federal aid programs, call 800-4-FED-AID.

Other Related Financial Aid Books

Annual Register of Grant Support. Chicago: Marquis, [annual].

A's and B's of Academic Scholarships. Alexandria, VA: Octameron, [annual].

Chronicle Student Aid Annual. Moravia, NY: Chronicle Guidance, [annual].

College Blue Book. Scholarships, Fellowships, Grants and Loans. New York: Macmillan, [annual].

College Financial Aid Annual. New York: Prentice-Hall, [annual].

Directory of Financial Aids for Minorities. San Carlos, CA: Reference Service Press, [biennial].

Directory of Financial Aids for Women. San Carlos, CA: Reference Service Press, [biennial].

Leider, Robert and Ann Leider. *Don't Miss Out: The Ambitious Student's Guide to Financial Aid*. Alexandria, VA: Octameron, [annual].

Financial Aids for Higher Education. Dubuque: Wm. C. Brown, [biennial].

Financial Aid for the Disabled and their Families. San Carlos, CA.: Reference Service Press, [biennial].

Peterson's Guides. *Paying Less for College*. Princeton, NJ: Peterson's, [annual].

INSIDE TRACK

Kenneth D. Riddle Jr.
Deputy Fire Chief
Las Vegas Fire & Rescue

While in high school I became interested in the medical profession as result of a class in which students were allowed to work in the local hospital. I liked it so much that I became a Red Cross volunteer and spent many hours working in various areas of the hospital, including the emergency room and the laboratory. In my senior year of high school, I applied for a job at the hospital and was hired as an Orderly (now called a Nursing Assistant). While working in the ER I decided to become an Emergency Medical Technician (EMT). I attended EMT training and was hired at age 18 by Mercy Ambulance in Las Vegas, and worked there from 1974 to 1978. In 1978, I started working with the Las Vegas Fire Department as a firefighter-paramedic. Since being hired I have also held the positions of EMS Training Officer (a Captain's rank), EMS Battalion Chief, Assistant Fire Chief, and Deputy Fire Chief.

I really liked being a firefighter-paramedic because you could actually help someone who needed assistance, especially when it involved life-saving assistance. It always made me feel good when I was able to save someone's life. Of course, I would get upset at not being able to save everyone. The long hours also became something to dislike as I got older.

As a Deputy Fire Chief, I am responsible for the medical aspects of the fire department, including the EMS program, health and wellness, and safety. I am also in charge of a new program the department is developing for responding to medical incidents resulting from the use of weapons of mass destruction. A typical shift for me begins at 8:00 A.M. Usually, I return phone calls in the morning, check my schedule for the day, and provide assistance to my staff. My current staff consists of a doctor, nurse, EMS Battalion Chief, a Fire Training Officer, and a Stress Management Coordinator. I get my job satisfaction in this position by helping my staff to be successful. I spend most of my time maintaining and enhancing current programs and planning new programs, of which there are many for the progressive fire department.

My advice to anyone interested in EMS or the fire service is to start young. Attend courses and programs and join organizations that are related to the field. You must have an advanced education to be competitive—the education often gives you an advantage during the application process, and it also improves your abilities and performance. The biggest change to the EMS and the fire service is the use of technology and the expansion of services. The technology available today makes the job of firefighting safer and the EMS tasks more reliable. Unfortunately this technology is often out of the financial reach of many agencies. Another major change is the role of the fire service today—modern fire service agencies do much more than just fight fires—from medical services and prevention education to social services and community programs, the fire service has changed a lot, and it will keep on changing and growing into the future.

CHAPTER five

SUCCEEDING ON THE JOB

YOU'RE READY to begin your career as a firefighter. This chapter will guide you from your first days as a "probie" to years down the road, when you're looking at promotions. The qualities of successful firefighters are explained, along with the steps you need to follow in order to move up in the ranks. Advancement opportunities and other fire-related career options are clearly explained.

CAREER FIREFIGHTERS, those who stay in the firefighting field until retirement, follow many of the same basic steps and have many of the same strengths. Learning the secrets of their success can be the first step in including yourself in their ranks. To start, you'll need to do well in your job as a probationary firefighter. It is only after you make it through the probationary period that you are fully admitted and sworn in as an official firefighter in good standing. Then you may become eligible for a wealth of advancement options, from attaining Firefighter II certification to becoming a lieutenant, captain, or fire chief. Several other fire-related career paths are open to you as well, from fire code enforcement officer to arson investigator and more. But it all begins with the probationary period.

SUCCEEDING AS A PROBATIONARY FIREFIGHTER

After you are hired by a fire department, you'll most likely begin a fire training course. In large urban fire departments, new recruits are normally trained for several weeks at the department's own training center. Smaller fire departments may send you to a state or county fire academy. Either way, this training is often considered "boot camp" for new firefighters. The physical demands are rigorous and may include a variety of tasks, such as using axes, saws, chemical extinguishers, ladders, and other equipment during simulated emergencies. Classroom work is normally required as well.

Training of new firefighters differs from state to state because some require job applicants to obtain Firefighter I certification before they can be hired, while others won't allow you to be certified as a firefighter until after you are hired. Regardless of the amount and intensity of the training you receive as a newly hired firefighter, you will learn the standard operating procedures (SOP) for your department and gain skills that should help to prepare you for success in your new career.

Fitting into the Fire House Culture

Newly hired firefighters undergo a period of probation, ranging from 6 to 18 months. Most "probies" get through this period and are sworn in as official firefighters, but it is also possible that either the firefighter or the hiring department may decide that he or she isn't cut out to be a firefighter. Therefore it is crucial that you do your best, apply yourself, foster a teamwork attitude, and follow orders during your probationary period.

In many fire departments, the practice of "breaking in the probies" is similar to the way fraternity members deal with new pledges. Essentially harmless taunting and practical joking are commonplace, and although it may be difficult, the best way to deal with it is to quickly develop a strong sense of humor. (We're not speaking here about dangerous hazing behavior, which is very rare and can be illegal.) You don't want to make enemies or get a reputation as someone who can't take a joke. Because teamwork is so important to firefighters, much of the teasing and the practical jokes are a way to "feel out" new firefighters to see how they'll take it and if they'll be a good sport about it.

Learning from Mentors

Finding and learning from a mentor can be an essential element in your success. A mentor is someone whom you identify as successful and with whom you create an informal teacher-student relationship. Enter into the relationship intending to observe your mentor carefully, and ask a lot of questions. The following is a list of things you may learn from a mentor:

▶ public interaction skills
▶ how to study for promotional exams
▶ what to expect in the fire house culture
▶ how to communicate with the chain of command in your department
▶ in-depth knowledge about equipment and technology used by your department
▶ helpful tips for repair and maintenance of equipment and supplies
▶ what are the best firefighter magazines and other resource materials
▶ what conferences, classes, or training programs you should attend

You'll probably need to actively search for a mentor in your fire house, unless someone decides to take you under his or her wing and show you the ropes. A mentor can be anyone from a battalion chief to one of your peers. There is no formula for who makes a good mentor; it is not based on title, level of seniority, or years in the department. Instead, the qualities of a good mentor are based on a combination of willingness to be a mentor, level of expertise in a certain area, teaching ability, and attitude.

When looking for a mentor, keep in mind the following questions:

▶ When asked a question, does the potential mentor take the time to help you find a resolution rather than point you toward someone else who can help you?
▶ Does the potential mentor tackle problems in a reasonable manner until they are resolved?

▶ What is it that people admire about the potential mentor? Do the admirable qualities coincide with your values and goals?

▶ Is he or she strong in areas in which you are weak?

Once you've entered into a relationship with a mentor, you should learn as much as you can from him or her. Keep in mind that, after a while, career growth may open up different possibilities in new areas of specialization. If that happens, you'll probably want to find additional mentors who can show you the ropes in the new environment. However, any former mentors you can keep as friends will not only help you with your career, but can also enrich your life. An experienced firefighter from San Jose, California, recollects the following about his first mentor:

> I'll never forget my first mentor in the fire department. I felt so green when I started, and I was afraid of messing up all the time. Then I sought out a senior firefighter who had been with the department for 18 years and began asking him simple questions about how things were run. He was a little gruff at first, but I think he was flattered that I asked him stuff. Pretty soon, he started telling me stories about how things worked around the place, and I got lots of tips and inside information about what the chief was like and how I should respond to the different firefighters and the captain on our shift. I'm still friends with him to this day, even though he retired a long time ago.

INTERACTING WITH SUPERVISORS

The most important action you can take to help you interact successfully with a supervisor, whether he or she is a captain or a battalion chief, an incident commander at the site of an emergency or a fire chief, is to follow that person's orders quickly and carefully. Due to the dangerous nature of fire fighting, following the orders of superior officers is of utmost importance. Some new firefighters think they can do things better than the way they are currently being done. Be careful about making any brash claims about how great your ideas are when you first begin your firefighting career. The best advice is to lie low for a while, finding out the motivations behind the orders and seeing the results of those orders in action.

When you're not in the midst of an emergency, there is a wide open field of how to best interact with your supervisors. Some fire stations have an informal atmosphere in which everyone interacts, regardless of rank. Other fire houses are more formal, and you need to be on your guard when addressing company officers. You'll get a feel for the atmosphere in your fire house after a few weeks on the job. Until you know for sure, play it safe by assuming a more formal manner when addressing your supervisors.

INTERACTING WITH THE PUBLIC

Public interaction is an important part of the firefighter's job. Whether it's in an emergency situation or during a public fire prevention talk, firefighters are highly respected. You don't want to do anything that might endanger that sense of respect. This is especially important during times of government downsizing and budget-cutting, when public support is crucial to the success of both municipal and volunteer fire departments.

One way in which fire departments can foster public support is through their collective, positive actions on emergency calls. Firefighters who offer help and comfort to victims in emergency situations, in addition to providing professional emergency assistance, generate good will from the citizens being helped as well as from people in the vicinity who witness such help. For example, firefighters who take the time to explain what is happening after a fire occurs or who retrieve someone's prized wedding album from wreckage can go a long way toward building respect and support in the community.

You'll find that many fire departments focus increasingly on good public relations during an emergency. It builds taxpayer support for municipal departments and healthier donations for volunteer departments. Being a conscientious worker and developing a high standard of work performance, along with displaying a caring attitude during emergencies, can be integral parts of your success as a firefighter.

DEVELOPING THE QUALITIES THAT COUNT

As you progress through your firefighting career, knowing the qualities that are rewarded will give you an edge. There are several things you can do to increase your educational background, technical skills, and effectiveness as a firefighter, as noted in Chapter 3. The personal qualities that are rewarded in fire departments follow the rules of common sense and include things such as

► honesty in your dealings with other firefighters, supervisors, and the public

► mental alertness, which, when you're on duty, can mean the difference between life and death

► respect for the chain of command; the incident commander at an emergency has the most information to insure the giving of proper orders

► compliance with safety precautions, in order to save lives and reduce injuries

► willingness to learn from mistakes; noting what went wrong during an emergency call, and analyzing why it did, can help to ensure that it doesn't happen again

► good listening skills; if important safety points and orders need to be repeated, time is wasted, which may cost lives

KNOWING WHEN TO BE READY

According to the U.S. Fire Administration, fire calls peak between 5 and 7 P.M. from the surge in cooking-related fires during the dinner period. Broken down by season, residential fires are most frequent during the winter, when heating is a dominant cause. For example, the residential fire rate for January is almost twice that of summer months, and the fire death rate for January is triple that of summer months.

MAINTAINING PERSONAL HEALTH AND FITNESS

Firefighters need to maintain good health and physical fitness in order to perform their tasks well. Some fire departments provide on-site facilities, such as weight training equipment or other fitness machines, to help firefighters stay in shape. If your department doesn't, consider joining a fitness center nearby or planning regular workouts with other firefighters. You may need to take and pass physical ability tests on a regular basis or in order to achieve a promotion in some fire departments, so you'll want to be ready.

Eating balanced meals and getting enough sleep are constant challenges to the modern firefighter. If you are on a work schedule in which you eat meals together at the fire house, suggest healthful alternatives to the regular diet. Your energy and stamina come from the food you eat, so it should be optimal fuel for your body. The right amount of sleep also affects energy and stamina, so you'll need to make a good effort to get the sleep hours you need.

JUST THE FACTS

In 1970, California firefighters established the Firefighter's Olympic Games as a way to promote physical fitness and have a friendly competition that could double as a casual convention of colleagues. The Firefighter's Olympics now boasts both summer and winter games, including such varied events as bowling, bass fishing, rodeo, and water skiing. The 2000 Firefighter's Summer Olympics were held in San Diego, California.

ADVANCEMENT OPPORTUNITIES

Some firefighters are very satisfied with their job and make fighting fires their lifelong career. Others may join up with a municipal fire department as a firefighter and then move into a position of higher rank, such as lieutenant or captain. The advancement route firefighters can pursue varies, depending on the size and location of their fire department, but usually follows this path: level-two firefighter, apparatus operator (or engineer), lieutenant or captain, battalion chief, assistant chief, deputy chief, and, finally, fire chief. Of course, not everyone advances to become a fire chief, but many firefighters do advance to the level of apparatus operator, lieutenant, or captain.

Advancement opportunities for firefighters often depend on several factors:

- ► seniority
- ► scores on promotional exams
- ► recommendations from supervisors
- ► job performance
- ► the number of openings in higher positions
- ► growth of the department
- ► education level

You may have all the qualifications, motivation, and skills needed for a promotion in your department, yet find that there are no openings at the next level. When that happens, you can either wait for an opening to occur or you can apply for a job in another fire department that has more advancement opportunities. According to a firefighter in Florida, it may be worth it to stay in your department and wait for an opening, if you really enjoy your work and the people you work with. He says:

I joined my department at a time when there were already several people who had just been promoted, so I had to wait nine years before I was able to land a promotion to apparatus operator. Then it was another eight years before I made it to lieutenant. Now I see guys getting promoted to those positions within only three or four years of being hired, because so many people are retiring or moving on now. It's really a cyclical thing, so if early promotion is extremely important to you, try to find out how many people have been promoted recently in your fire department. If it doesn't look good, you may want to try and transfer to another department right away, before you get too settled in. However, if you don't mind the wait, there's great security in staying where you are and not moving around.

You may want to consider applying to another fire department for a number of reasons. Realize that by getting a job in another fire department, you can, in essence, give yourself a promotion. Even if it's a lateral move, you may enjoy one or more of these benefits from a move:

▶ better pay
▶ preferable health benefits and work schedule
▶ superior training programs
▶ improved firefighting equipment
▶ better camaraderie with coworkers and supervisors
▶ more room for advancement

Of course, if you land your first job in a great fire department that offers many benefits and advancement opportunities, then you're all set. You can focus on learning all you can and preparing yourself for future promotional opportunities or career challenges in related areas. Should you decide to seek advancement in the firefighting field, the promotion process is explained below.

How to Prepare for a Promotion

Many experienced firefighters study regularly to improve their job performance and prepare for promotion examinations. In general, firefighters today need more training to operate increasingly sophisticated equipment and to deal safely with the greater hazards associated with fighting fires in larger, more elaborate structures. To progress to higher-level positions, firefighters need to acquire expertise in the most advanced fire-fighting equipment and techniques, building construction, emergency medical procedures, writing, public speaking, management, budgeting procedures, and labor relations.

IN THE NEWS

Considered one of the best advancements in fire-fighting equipment in recent years, the thermal imaging camera allows firefighters to detect people when they cannot see them. The cameras distinguish items of various temperatures within a room, leading rescuers to human victims in rooms filled with thick smoke. They can also show firefighters where the fire's hot spots are, where the most intense effort is needed, without the firefighters having to break through a structure. The downside? Thermal imaging cameras cost up to $25,000 each.

Fire departments frequently conduct training programs, several colleges and schools offer fire science training programs, and the National Fire Academy sponsors relevant training programs on various topics, including executive development, anti-arson techniques, and public fire safety and education. Some states also provide extensive firefighting training programs at all levels. For instance, in Maryland, the Maryland Fire Service Personnel Qualifications Board offers training and certification for several areas of specialization, including but not limited to:

Driver/Operator	Fire Instructor I, II, III, IV
Airport Firefighter	Haz Mat Responder
Fire Officer I, II, III, IV	Haz Mat Technician
Fire Inspector I, II, III	Haz Mat Incident Commander
Fire Investigator	EMS Haz Mat I, II
Public Fire Educator I, II, III	Advanced Exterior Fire Brigade

Taking Promotional Exams

Once you've decided to try for a particular promotion, you'll need to set up a plan for obtaining that goal. Several things can help your chances of scoring high on a promotional exam, as follows:

1. Get an idea of what will be on the promotional exam. You can ask people who have already taken the exam what areas were emphasized and what books they recommend that you study in order to prepare for the exam. You may be able to get old tests that have been published for students to review. You may even be fortunate enough to get a suggested reading list along with the exam materials, although this is rare.
2. Set priorities on what material to study. You can't possibly learn every detail about the job, so focus on the most important aspects. This will

help prevent your getting bogged down in details that are not going to be tested on the promotional exam.

3. Study test preparation books to find out or brush up on the skills needed to succeed on written exams. For example, look up information on how to handle test anxiety, how to score as high as possible on multiple-choice questions, and how to take tests within specific time limits. See Appendix C at the end of this book for resources.

4. Make a study schedule several months before the exam, and stick to it. Allow sufficient time each day for studying a section of material, and don't forget to preview and review the material you study each day. A good study method is to create flash cards and test yourself on key concepts and questions you think may appear on the test.

5. Find out if your fire department uses assessment centers to test practical, hands-on aspects of the job you are applying for. If so, talk to people who have gone through the assessment center to get their advice on how you can prepare for this segment of the process. You should also find out if you are allowed to tour the assessment facility to get an idea of what equipment will be used to test you.

JOB DESCRIPTIONS FOR ADVANCED POSITIONS

To get a better idea of where your future firefighting career could lead you, read the following job descriptions of key advancement opportunities in the field.

The following salaries are for full-time, sworn-in personnel and were gathered from a nationwide survey.

Position	Minimum Annual Base Salary	Maximum Annual Base Salary
Firefighter	$26,900	$35,200
Fire Lieutenant	$32,200	$39,800
Fire Captain	$35,100	$44,700
Assistant Fire Chief	$43,900	$53,200
Battalion Chief	$45,300	$56,000
Deputy Chief	$45,900	$56,900
Fire Chief	$52,700	$66,000

Apparatus Operator

Apparatus operators drive the fire truck to emergency calls. They are also referred to as engineers or chauffeurs in some departments. Their skill level goes well beyond merely driving the fire truck, however. They also maintain, inspect, and perform minor repairs on emergency vehicles to ensure a high level of performance. They are responsible for operating pumps, aerial ladders, and/or other equipment during fire suppression calls. Various national certifications for this position are available, including the following:

▶ Driver/Operator—Pumper
▶ Driver/Operator—Aerial
▶ Driver/Operator—Tiller
▶ Driver/Operator—ARF
▶ Driver/Operator—Wildland

Apparatus operators are paid a higher salary than firefighters due to their specialized knowledge and greater amount of responsibility.

Lieutenant or Captain

Lieutenants and captains are referred to as company officers. They supervise firefighters and issue orders to their crew at the scene of emergencies. The size of each lieutenant or captain's crew varies considerably, depending on the size and location of the fire department. However, they all need to be well versed in how to handle emergency situations and how to manage personnel, as these two activities make up a large portion of their job. They may also be responsible for training new firefighters in fire house procedures, inspecting fire house equipment, and making requests for additional or newer equipment. Lieutenants and captains are normally paid considerably more than firefighters (at least 20–25%), due to their higher level of responsibility and added management duties.

Battalion Chief

Battalion chiefs hold the next highest rank after lieutenants and captains. They are responsible for a group of lieutenants and captains as well as the firefighters who work under them. Battalion chiefs coordinate and supervise the fire companies under their command during emergency calls and keep communication lines open between lieutenants or captains and superior officers. They are often responsible for recommending personnel for awards; inspecting records, equipment, and personnel in their jurisdiction; issuing purchase orders; and preparing reports of accidents or other noteworthy incidents. They may also assist the fire chief in creating and maintaining departmental budgets and other administrative tasks as needed. Battalion chiefs earn approximately 10–15% more than lieutenants or captains because of the higher level of responsibility involved in their job.

Deputy Fire Chief or Assistant Fire Chief

Deputy or assistant fire chiefs perform many of the same functions as the fire chief. They are found mostly in large urban fire departments, because fire chiefs need help in departments that employ large numbers of firefighters and cover densely populated areas. Some deputy fire chiefs are responsible for a particular sector of the department, such as operations or training, or they may cover a particular district. See the description under the fire chief category below for the types of duties that many deputy and assistant chiefs perform.

Fire Chief

The fire chief is on the top rung of the career ladder for firefighters. Fire chiefs are responsible for entire fire departments, including all firefighters, lieutenants, captains, battalion chiefs, and any deputy or assistant fire chiefs. Therefore their duties are numerous and varied. The specific job duties of fire chiefs depend on the size and type of fire department they are managing. In general, fire chiefs are normally responsible for managing the resources of the department, preparing the departmental budget, commanding multiple-alarm fires, administering laws and regulations in their department, and acting as liaison for the fire department with public officials. Salaries for fire chiefs vary greatly. A fire chief in charge of several thousand firefighters is going to command a much higher salary than one who manages a staff of fewer than a hundred. Many fire chiefs earn a significant salary due to their many years of experience and high level of education. Some earn close to or even over $100,000 annually. Of course, fire chiefs in small rural areas earn considerably less.

Sample Job Postings for Advanced Positions

These postings can give you an idea of the requirements and salaries available with advancement opportunities. Of course, salaries vary considerably depending on location and size of the fire department, but these descriptions can give you a good idea of what to expect.

Position:	Firefighter/Paramedic
Location:	Florida
Requirements:	State of Florida firefighter certification from the Bureau of Fire Standards and Training; current state of Florida paramedic certification (or proof of enrollment as a third semester-paramedic student)
Salary:	$33,411–48,389 (includes paramedic assignment pay)
Position:	Safety Division Manager/Fire Marshal
Location:	Oregon
Description:	Responsible for the fire department's Safety Division, which includes all operations related to the prevention of fire and life safety issues for the public and any related safety issues for the fire department employees; coordinates and organizes logistical aspects of the department's needs; and does related work as required
Requirements:	Associate's degree in emergency services field (bachelor's degree preferred); 10 years' experience in fire service, with

background in fire prevention, fire codes and ordinances, training, budgeting, field supervision, and planning; state-certified Fire Officer I; state-certified EMT-B; possession of valid state driver's license; must pass physical exam, including drug testing, and be a nonsmoker

Salary: $52,068–64,032

Position: Fire Protection Engineer

Location: California

Description: Participates directly in the review of building and development plans for compliance with state and local fire codes and other permit requirements, conducts highly technical fire prevention activities, and provides highly technical staff assistance

Requirements: Equivalent of a bachelor's degree, with major in fire protection engineering or a closely related field; sufficient fire prevention and plan review experience to demonstrate knowledge of principles of modern fire prevention, fire protection engineering, and fire suppression activities, knowledge of fire codes and applicable state laws; and ability to make studies and prepare reports, enforce codes, ordinances and regulations, and represent the fire department to contractors, engineers, architects, and developers

Salary: $69,588–84,528

Position: Fire Chief

Location: Arizona

Description: Plans, directs, and controls departmental activities, including recruitment of personnel, purchase of equipment, and assignment of personnel and equipment; coordinates activities with other town departments and outside agencies to ensure effective working relationships and mutual aid agreements; develops appropriate contract documents for administrative and operational needs and routinely upgrades them; evaluates needs and makes recommendations for location and construction of fire stations and purchase of apparatus and equipment; conducts, supervises, and reviews the town's fire department in-service training program; resolves citizen complaints and problems concerning activities of the department; and coordinates with code

	enforcement in the development, revision, and enforcement of town fire and building codes.
Requirements:	Bachelor's degree in fire science, public administration, or business administration; a minimum of eight years of increasingly responsible command and supervisory experience in a professional municipal fire department; five years' experience as chief, deputy chief, or assistant chief preferred
Salary:	$73,505–101,518

CAREER OPTIONS

Fire service is a broad and still-expanding field that offers numerous career choices. In general, firefighter training offers a good basic background for other fire service careers. Certain career paths involve returning to college or even graduate school for more in-depth study of subjects such as biology and chemistry only touched upon by firefighting academies. There are also "civilian" career paths in fire service that have specific higher education or certification requirements but don't necessarily require firefighter training.

Here are descriptions of several fire-related careers. Note that some options require several years of firefighting experience, while others require highly specialized training.

Fire Prevention Specialists

Fire prevention specialists work with a variety of people to teach fire prevention techniques. Many lecture at schools, nonprofit groups, civic organizations, and senior living residences. They also work with home and business owners to ensure that vegetation around buildings and homes are cut down and that open spaces between structures are not overgrown with long, dry grass—the fuel of those large wildfires that plague many parts of the country every year.

The priorities for prevention programs are tailored to different locations and purposes. Fire prevention specialists teach people the leading causes of fires—cooking, heating, and arson—and what the leading causes of fire deaths are: careless smoking, heating, and arson. These causes are relatively similar around the nation.

Typical Minimum Requirements

The minimum requirements for the position of fire prevention specialist vary from department to department. Some fire departments require that these positions be filled with experienced firefighters through a promotion and application process, which could take several years to complete. Other fire departments open the position of fire prevention specialist to graduates of fire science degree programs who haven't ever served as firefighters. Fire prevention specialists normally have some formal education, public speaking skills, and teaching experience in their background.

Fire Code Enforcement Officers

Fire code enforcement officers oversee the more technical aspects of fire prevention and are similar to fire inspectors. They often review building plans to designate and ensure compliance with fire safety codes and protection systems. They also assess the number and placement of fire exits and establish the maximum number of occupants allowed in a building. Some states refer to their fire inspectors as fire code enforcement officers, while others differentiate between the two.

Typical Minimum Requirements

Minimum requirements for becoming a fire code enforcement officer vary among departments and states. However, applicants normally need to have either sufficient training from a recognized training program or several years of experience in the field before attaining the level of fire code enforcement officer.

Fire Marshals

The duties of fire marshals vary greatly depending on what state they work in. The fire marshal in some states may be appointed by one of the following:

▶ a state's attorney general
▶ a state fire board
▶ a fire prevention commission
▶ other governing body

Many fire marshals serve as investigators and investigate fires to determine their origin, whether fire laws have been violated, and whether a fire is the result of criminal negligence or arson. In some states, fire marshals are given powers of subpoena and arrest to investigate the cause of a fire. Marshals may test sites for flammable gases or liquids and are trained to evaluate burn patterns to show where a fire started and how it burned. They report their findings to the district attorney if criminal charges should be filed and are often familiar with laws and court procedures. Many fire marshals also perform inspections of commercial buildings to enforce state fire prevention codes and perform other administrative duties.

Typical Minimum Requirements

The minimum requirements for becoming a fire marshal vary greatly nationwide. In most states, they are required to have extensive experience in fire service and public safety or related areas. Consult the sample job postings beginning on page 162 for the requirements specified by a fire department in Oregon.

Arson Investigators

Arson investigators may work in conjunction with the fire marshal's office or in a fire department's fire prevention division. They investigate the causes of fires and explosions to find out if criminal activity was involved. Their investigative responsibilities are often similar to those performed by fire marshals in some states. Arson investigators use their analytical skills and knowledge of fire science to make judgments and create reports about the fires they investigate. Many arson investigators interview relevant parties to determine the probable cause of a fire. They sometimes testify as expert witnesses in court cases.

Typical Minimum Requirements

Arson investigators are often promoted from a position within a fire department or fire prevention division. Therefore they often possess firefighting skills or knowledge of fire science practices and procedures. Some states may hire investigators from fire-related fields other than firefighting. Specialized knowledge in how fires are started and how they spread is needed. Organization and analytical skills are also helpful. Most arson investigators have some level of college training.

Hazardous Materials Specialists

Firefighters who deal with dangerous situations involving hazardous materials, called "haz mat" in the field, require specialized training and equipment. Therefore fire departments usually employ specially trained personnel who are called in to clean up spills or leaks such as deadly waste dumped from refineries and chemical or nuclear plants.

This growing field is heavily regulated by state and national agencies and requires proper certification, which can be achieved through extension programs at many public colleges. In addition to college training courses, many fire departments take it upon themselves to train their "haz mat" personnel in their own safety and emergency-response procedures.

Typical Minimum Requirements

Certification in hazardous materials often involves a combination of hands-on and classroom learning from a fire academy, community college, or correspondence course. Some programs offer different levels of certification in hazardous materials, such as

- ▶ Haz Mat Responder—Awareness
- ▶ Haz Mat Responder—Operational
- ▶ Haz Mat—Technician
- ▶ Haz Mat Incident Commander
- ▶ Haz Mat Off-Site Specialist, Employees

Crash, Fire, and Rescue Firefighters

Specialized knowledge is needed to become an airport firefighter who deals with airplane crashes and fires. These firefighters conduct rescue efforts of plane crews and passengers in the event of an emergency. They may respond to potential air crash emergencies, by spraying foam on the runway to minimize the chances of an explosion, or to actual air crash emergencies by spraying chemical solutions or water fog onto the aircraft. They offer emergency medical procedures to victims and may be involved in deactivating aircraft electrical power to prevent explosions. Crash, fire, and rescue firefighters may be employed by commercial, military, or general airports.

Typical Minimum Requirements

Firefighters who want to specialize in the crash, fire, and rescue area need to obtain training and experience to prepare them for the intricacies of the job. Training programs are offered throughout the nation to help firefighters learn the specialized information needed to respond to air crash, fire, and rescue needs at airports. Firefighters can become certified as an airport firefighter by meeting the standards set by the National Board on Fire Service Professional Qualifications, a division of the National Fire Protection Association (NFPA).

Fire Insurance Company Representatives

Several hiring opportunities are available for firefighters, or others interested in the firefighting field, are in fire insurance companies. For example, fire insurance claim examiners are needed to analyze claims, decide which are valid, and in some cases settle claims after reviewing available data and interviewing both claimants and agents.

Claims adjusters are also needed in the fire insurance area. They are responsible for negotiating settlements after inspecting property damage and other incidents related to a fire. Adjusters usually have to prepare comprehensive reports about each case they get.

A third insurance company representative is the fire science specialist, who may help the insurance company set rates for fire-related coverage. He or she may also examine fire prevention methods, such as sprinkler systems, at various places of business and offer suggestions for improving hazardous conditions.

Typical Minimum Requirements

There are no hard-and-fast rules about who can become a fire insurance company representative. Due to the variety of employers, people with a variety of backgrounds and requirements are needed. In general, you'll need some training or background in fire science and fire investigation work. Some companies may offer you on-the-job-training to fill in the gaps in your background. Many companies look favorably on applicants who have completed an associate's degree in fire science or a related area.

Fire Services Instructors

Firefighters who are interested in education may wish to become instructors within their fire departments or at a nearby community college or other fire training school. Instructors who work in fire departments are often called training officers. They provide training to all levels of firefighters, from new recruits to senior firefighters who need help with new materials. Rank depends on the size and location of the fire department, but instructors are often at the level of captain or higher.

In addition to teaching in a classroom or lab facility, instructors may also organize training programs for specific groups of people or specific tasks. For example, they may need to organize a training program for newly hired recruits or for firefighters who want to apply for the position of apparatus operator or lieutenant. Instructors at colleges or fire academies perform similar teaching functions and may be involved in organizing or updating training programs.

Typical Minimum Requirements

Since firefighter instructors need a wealth of knowledge in order to teach others, they must have a solid foundation in the subject matter they are teaching. Therefore they would benefit from several years of working as a firefighter before becoming an instructor. For instructors in specialized fields, such as hazardous materials or crash and rescue operations, additional education and field experience are needed. Instructors can obtain certification according to standards set by the National Fire Protection Association (NFPA).

Wildland Smoke Jumper Supervisors

Smoke jumper supervisors coordinate airborne firefighting crews during wildland fires. They examine the location, size, and condition of a wildfire, so they know how many smoke jumpers to employ in each area of the fire. They oversee the process of dropping equipment from aircraft to the smoke jumpers on the ground as well as retrieving smoke jumpers from the field after a fire is placed under control. Smoke jumper supervisors may be involved in combating actual fires along with their subordinates. They maintain open lines of communication between the smoke jumpers in the field and the crews back at the base of operations. They also train new smoke jumpers in

- ▶ parachute jumping
- ▶ wildland fire suppression
- ▶ aerial observation of fires
- ▶ radio communications

Typical Minimum Requirements
Smoke jumper supervisors need extensive experience both as smoke jumpers and as wildland firefighters. Since it may take several years to land a job as a smoke jumper, due to the extremely intense physical fitness level required and the competitive nature of the job, people may need to serve for several years as a seasonal wildland firefighter before becoming a smoke jumper.

Forest Fire Warden or Fire Ranger

Fire wardens and rangers are needed in forests and other wildland areas to take fire prevention measures and to scout for dangerous fire conditions.

They perform inspections of campsites, logging areas, and other remote areas to help prevent and to report fires. In the case of a forest fire, they may become crew leaders and issue commands on the fire line and in the base camp. They normally examine and maintain firefighting equipment and supplies to ensure accordance with company and government regulations. They may need to give first aid to accident victims.

Typical Minimum Requirements

Typical minimum requirements for a fire warden or ranger depend on whether you want to work on state, federal, or private lands. Many forest fire wardens and deputies have experience as seasonal wildland firefighters, and they become certified through various agencies.

Succeeding in Every Step of Your Career

Now that you've learned about many of the advancement opportunities available to firefighters, it's time to think seriously about the direction you'd like your career to take. Some people working in fire services prefer to remain firefighters, in on all the action, until retirement. Others work up the ranks toward fire chief or get hired out of the fire house as investigators, insurance experts, or instructors teaching the next generation of firefighters.

We've outlined the steps you need to follow if you think you might seek a promotion. Do some further research into any or all of the advanced positions that interest you. Even in the first days of your career, you can begin to follow a path toward the future.

INSIDE TRACK

Tom Guldner
New York City Fire Department (FDNY)
Lieutenant-Marine Division Training Officer
President, Marine Firefighting Institute

My family has a history with the FDNY and the NYPD. I actually started as a police officer, and after two years I learned that I had passed the firefighter exam and I switched to the FDNY. After 10 years of working in the South Bronx, I was promoted to lieutenant, after which I spent 10 more years in another of New York City's poorer neighborhoods, Washington Heights in Manhattan. Eight years ago I transferred to the marine division as a lieutenant on the department's only full-time marine fire/rescue boat.

I love my job. At times it has left me emotionally drained and physically weakened, but I wouldn't trade professions with anyone. The only things I'd like to change are the several injuries I've suffered and the fact that I've had to bury too many of my friends.

A typical day for me begins at 9 A.M. I conduct a roll call of everyone working that tour and assign duties and discuss any matters of importance. After paperwork and "committee work," which consists of cleaning the fire house, tools, and boat, we either go out on surveillance inspections of some of the city's piers, wharves, and waterside facilities or we try to board one of the many vessels in New York harbor for shipboard familiarization training. Some special duties include standing by whenever any dignitaries arrive at or depart from the port, as well as covering fireworks and water displays. Of course, we also respond to boat fires, boats in distress, and water rescues. The majority of my time is spent on training, water rescues, and marine firefighting.

The field has really changed since I began—I go way back. When I first joined the FDNY we were still being dispatched by telegraph bell signals. Masks were a novelty, and usually only one member of the company would wear one. We had no medical training and didn't perform any of the more specialized rescue activities. Back then we got the job done, but I'm glad to see some of the new innovations being introduced.

If you want to be a firefighter, the first thing to do is to check with the department you want to join to determine what skills, licenses, and training you must have. The entrance exams all consist of a written test and a physical test. There are many books and study classes that will help you prepare for the written portion, and you will have to be in top shape for the physical portion.

Appendix A

Employment Sources: Industry-Specific Recruiters and Internet Job Sites

INDUSTRY-SPECIFIC RECRUITERS

Careers in Fire Service
PO Box 778
Millbrae, CA 94030
800-997-3373
www.usfirejobs.com and www.firerecruit.com

Firehire
PO Box 1822
Elk Grove, CA 95759
800-755-5891
www.firehire.com
Firehire offers job descriptions, benefits, training information, and recruitment services for a fee to potential firefighters looking for a job.

International Fire and Police Recruitment Administration
1127 South Mannheim Road, Suite 203
Westchester, IL 60154
800-343-HIRE
www.ifpra.org

Public Safety Recruitment
PO Box 587
East Jordan, MI 49727
800-880-9018
www.psrjobs.com

The Perfect Firefighter Candidate
4475 Dupont Court, Suite #3
Ventura, CA 93003
800-326-8401
Fax 805-658-7128
www.firecareers.com

INTERNET JOB SITES

Fire Career Assistance Biweekly Job Listing Newsletter Subscription Site
www.firecareerassist.com

Firefighter.com Job Search Page
www.firefighter.com/jobsearch.cfm

Firefighter Jobs
home.pacbell.net/putt1234

Fire-Rescue Village Jobs Page
www.firevillage.com/career_center/jobs/index.cfm

The Fire Station
home.flash.net/~jturner/jobs.htm

National Directory of Emergency Services
www1.firejobs.com/ndes/

Federal Jobs Digest
www.jobsfed.com/rp/cgi/BrowzHow.cgi?GroupID=07&Series=0081&
    Valued=1
    If you are looking for a wildland fire-fighting job from the federal gov-
    ernment, you might want to check out this website. Select "Live Jobs,"
    then "Law Enforcement/Fire," and then "Fire Protection and
    Prevention" to see a list of federal fire-related job postings.

USA Jobs

www.usajobs.opm.gov

This federal government jobs website includes federal wildland firefighting job opportunities. It is a service provided by the Office of Personnel Management (OPM).

Appendix B

Government Agencies, Professional Associations, Unions, and Educational Accrediting Agencies

GOVERNMENT AGENCIES, PROFESSIONAL ASSOCIATIONS, AND UNIONS

Fire and Aviation Management Program
U.S. Forest Service
U.S. Department of Agriculture
PO Box 96090
Washington, D.C. 20090-6090
703-235-3220
www.fs.fed.us/fire

Fire Department Safety Officers Association
PO Box 149
Ashland, MA 01721-0149
508-881-3114
www.fdsoa.org/

International Association of Arson
Investigators
12770 Boenker Road
St. Louis, MO 63044
314-739-4224
www.fire-investigators.org

International Association of Black
Professional Fire Fighters
8700 Central Avenue, Suite 306
Landover, MD 20785
301-808-0804
www.iabpff.org

International Association of Fire Chiefs
4025 Fair Ridge Drive, Suite 300
Fairfax, VA 22033-2868
703-273-0911
www.ichiefs.org/contact/index.html

International Association of Fire Fighters
1750 New York Avenue NW
Washington, DC 20006
202-737-8484
www.iaff.org/iaff/index.html

International Association for Fire Safety
Science
c/o SFPE
7315 Wisconsin Avenue, Suite 1225W
Bethesda, MD 20814
E-mail: sfpehqtrs@sfpe.org
www.iafss.org
The Website for the International
Association for Fire Safety Science (IAFSS)
offers information of interest to firefighters.
The association offers a newsletter, encourages research in the science of preventing
fires, holds meetings, and has an active
membership. Contact Kathleen Almand.

International Association of Wildland Fire
PO Box 328
Fairfield, WA 99012
509-523-4003
www.wildfiremagazine.com

International Fire Service Training
Association
IFSTA/Fire Service Programs
930 North Willis
Stillwater, OK 74078-8045
800-654-4055
-or-
405-744-5723
www.ifsta.org

International Society of Fire Service
Instructors
1259 Courthouse Road
Stafford, VA 22554
800-435-0005

E-mail: info@isfsi.org
www.isfsi.org
The International Society of Fire Service
Instructors (ISFSI) offers a monthly maga-
zine.

Los Angeles Fire Recruitment
212-847-LAFD
24-hour job hotline 213-847-9424
www.ci.la.ca.us/dept/PER/lafd.htm
The City of Los Angeles Fire Recruitment
Website discusses the application process
and minimum requirements for becoming a
firefighter in L.A. You can also call for an
application.

National Association of State Fire Marshals
1245 Farmington Avenue, Suite 101
West Hartford, CT 06107
877-996-2736
www.firemarshals.org
The National Association of State Fire
Marshals (NASFM) is an organization that
works to increase public awareness of the
dangers of fire. There are hotel and home
safety tips and information on sprinklers,
sprinkler ordinances, and smoke and heat
detectors on its Website.

National Association of State Foresters
444 North Capitol NW, Suite 540
Washington, DC 20001
www.stateforesters.com

National Fire Protection Association
1 Batterymarch Park
PO Box 9101
Quincy, MA 02269-9101
617-770-3000
www.nfpa.org

National Interagency Fire Center
3833 South Development Avenue
Boise, ID 83705-5354
208-387-5512
www.nifc.gov

National Volunteer Fire Council
1050 17th Street NW
Washington, DC 20036
888-ASK-NVFC
E-mail: nvfcoffice@nvfc.org
www.nvfc.org/state.html
The Website for the National Volunteer Fire
Council (NVFC), a nonprofit organization
offers news releases and other information
related to volunteer fire fighting.

Society of Fire Protection Engineers
7315 Wisconsin Avenue, Suite 1225 W
Bethesda, MD 20814
301-718-2910
www.sfpe.org

United States Fire Administration
16825 South Seton Avenue
Emmitsburg, MD 21727
301-447-1000
www.usfa.fema.gov

Western Fire Chiefs Association
300 North Main Street, #25
Fallbrook, CA 92028
760-723-6911
www.wfca.com

Women in the Fire Service
PO Box 5446
Madison, WI 53705
608-233-4768
www.wfsi.org

EDUCATIONAL ACCREDITING AGENCIES

National

Accrediting Commission for Career Schools and Colleges of Technology
2101 Wilson Boulevard, Suite 302
Arlington, VA 22201
703-247-4212
www.accsct.org

Accrediting Council for Independent
Colleges and Schools
750 First Street NE, Suite 980
Washington, DC 20002-4241
202-336-6780
www.acics.org

Distance Education and Training Council
1601 18th Street NW
Washington, DC 20009-2529
202-234-5100
www.detc.org

Regional

Middle States Association of Colleges and
Schools
Commission on Institutions of Higher
Education
3624 Market Street
Philadelphia, PA 19104
215-662-5606
www.msache.org

New England Association of Schools and
Colleges
Commission on Institutions of Higher
Education
209 Burlington Road
Bedford, MA 01730-1433
781-271-0022
www.neasc.org/cihe/cihe.htm

New England Association of Schools and
Colleges
Commission on Vocational, Technical, and
Career Institutions
209 Burlington Rd
Bedford, MA 01730-1433
781-271-0022
www.neasc.org/ctci/ctci.htm

North Central Association of Schools and
Colleges
Commission on Institutions of Higher
Education
30 North LaSalle Street, Suite 2400
Chicago, IL 60602-2504
800-621-7440
www.ncacihe.org

Northwest Association of Schools and
Colleges
Commission on Colleges
1910 University Drive
Boise, ID 83725-1060
208-426-5727
www2.idbsu.edu/nasc

Southern Association of Colleges and
Schools
Commission on Colleges
1866 Southern Lane
Decatur, GA 30033
404-679-4500
www.sacscoc.org

Western Association of Schools and
Colleges
Accrediting Commission for Community and
Junior Colleges
3402 Mendocino Avenue
Santa Rosa, CA 95403
707-569-9177
www.accjc.org

Western Association of Schools and
Colleges
Accrediting Commission for Senior Colleges
and Universities
985 Atlantic Avenue, Suite 100
Alameda, CA 94501
510-748-9001
www.wascweb.org/senior/wascsr.html

Appendix C

Additional Resources: College Guides, Distance Learning Resources, Career-Related Resources, Financial Aid and Scholarships, Firefighting Resources, Test Prep Materials, Skill Builders

COLLEGE GUIDES

The College Board College Handbook 2001. New York: The College Board, 2000.

Peterson's 2 Year Colleges 2001. Princeton, NJ: Peterson's, 2000.

Vocational & Technical Schools Set 2000, (2 vols). Princeton, NJ: Peterson's, 1999.

DISTANCE LEARNING RESOURCES

Distance Learning 2000. Princeton, NJ: Peterson's, 2000.

Criscito, Pat. *Barron's Guide to Distance Learning: Degrees, Certificates, Courses*. Hauppauge, NY: Barron's Educational Series, 1999.

Williams, Marcia L., Kenneth Paprock, and Barbara Covington. *Distance Learning: The Essential Guide*. Thousand Oaks, CA: Sage Publications, 1999.

Thorson, Marcie K. *Campus Free College Degrees: Thorsons Guide to Accredited College Degrees through Distance Learning*. Tulsa, OK: Thorson Guides, 2000.

CAREER-RELATED RESOURCES

Beatty, Richard H. *The Perfect Cover Letter*, 2nd ed. New York: John Wiley & Sons, 1997.

Great Interview. New York: LearningExpress, 2000.

Great Resume. New York: LearningExpress, 2000.

Occupational Outlook Handbook, 2000–01 ed. U.S. Bureau of Labor Statistics. Available on-line at www.bls.gov/ocohome.htm.

FINANCIAL AID AND SCHOLARSHIPS (BOOKS AND WEBSITES)

Books

Cassidy, David J. *The Scholarship Book: The Complete Guide to Private-Sector Scholarships, Fellowships, Grants, and Loans for the Undergraduate.* Upper Saddle River, NJ: Prentice Hall, 2000.

Peterson's Scholarships, Grants, and Prizes 2001. Lawrenceville, NJ: Peterson's, 2000.

The Complete Scholarship Book. Skokie, Ill.: SourceBooks/Fastweb.com, 2000.

Websites

FastWeb!—Helping Over 7 Million Students Find Scholarships, Colleges and Jobs!
www.fastweb.com

FinAid! The SmartStudent™ Guide to Financial Aid
www.finaid.org

GrantsNet (source for information on science and medical education)
www.grantsnet.org

List of All U.S. Government Programs Benefiting Students
www.fedmoney.org

Student Loan Finance Association
www.slfaloan.com

U.S. Department of Education Federal Student Financial Aid Homepage
www.ed.gov/offices/OSFAP/Students

Yahoo! Financial Aid page
dir.yahoo.com/education/financial_aid

FIREFIGHTING RESOURCES (BOOKS, PERIODICALS, AND WEBSITES)

Books

Carter, Harry R., and Lynne Murnane, eds. *Firefighting Strategy and Tactics.* Fire Protection Publications, 1998.

Delsohn, Steve. *The Fire Inside: Firefighters Talk about Their Lives.* New York: HarperCollins, 1996.

Dunn, Vincent. *Collapse of Burning Buildings: A Guide to Fireground Safety.* Fire Engineering Book Dept, 1987.

Hall, Richard, ed. *Essentials of Fire Fighting.* International Fire Service Training Association, 1998.

Norman, John. *Fire Officer's Handbook of Tactics.* Tulsa, OK: Pennwell Publishing, 1998.

Pyne, Stephen J. *Fire on the Rim: A Firefighter's Season at the Grand Canyon.* Seattle: University of Washington Press, 1995.

Teie, William C. *Firefighter's Handbook on Wildland Firefighting.* Rescue, CA: Deer Valley Press, 1994.

Periodicals

American Fire Journal
9072 East Artesia Boulevard, Suite 7
Bellflower, CA 90706
562-866-1664

Aviation Fire Journal
PO Box 976
Baldwin Place, NY 10505
www.aviationfirejournal.com

Fire Chief
307 North Michigan Avenue
Chicago, IL 60604
312-726-7277
www.firechief.com

Fire Engineering
875 Third Avenue
New York, NY 10022
212-845-0800
www.fire-eng.com

FireHouse
445 Broad Hollow Road
Melville, NY 11747
516-845-2700
www.firehouse.com

Fire Technology and *National Fire Protection Association Journal*
National Fire Protection Association
1 Batterymarch Park
PO Box 9101
Quincy, MA 02269-9101
617-770-3000
www.nfpa.org

National Fire and Rescue
3000 Highwoods Boulevard, Suite 300
Raleigh, NC 27604-1029
919-872-5040
www.nfrmag.com

Wildland Firefighter
PO Box 11809
Prescott, AZ 86304-1809
520-636-8000
wildlandfirefighter.com

Websites

Fire Service Testing Company, Inc.
www.fstc.com
This website offers information about fire and emergency service personnel testing for entrance and promotional exams. Services include written tests, test software, question banks, and assessments. On-line practice tests are available for a fee.

National Wildfire Coordinating Group (NWCG)
fire.nifc.nps.gov/mats/matsframe.asp
NWCG's computerized Multi-Agency Fire Training Schedule is a list of wildland fire and aviation training courses taught throughout the United States. Courses are hosted by federal, state, and local cooperating agencies. The site is your gateway to all wildland fire training. The schedule is compiled and updated daily at the National Interagency Fire Center (NIFC) in Boise, Idaho, and is hosted on the U.S. Department of the Interior's National Park Service (NPS) Fire Home Page (www.nifc.nps.gov/fire)

About.com Firefighting Webring Guide
http://firefighting.about.com/careers/firefighting/library/blwebrings.htm?rnk=r5&terms=EMS

The Fire and EMS (Emergency Medical Services) Information Network
www.fire-ems.net

Fire-Rescue Village
www.firevillage.com

Wildland Firefighters Resource Page
www.geocities.com/yosemite/gorge/5561

The Firefighters Page
www.workingfire.net

The United States Fire Administration National Fire Academy Degrees at
    a Distance program
www.usfa.fema.gov/nfa/tr_ddp.htm

Yahoo! Fire protection site
dir.yahoo.com/health/public_health_and_safety/fire_protection

TEST PREP MATERIALS

LearningExpress. *Firefighter Exam*. New York: LearningExpress, 2000.
———*Firefighter Exam California*. New York: LearningExpress, 1997.
———*Firefighter Exam Midwest*. New York: LearningExpress, 1997.
———*Firefighter Exam New Jersey*. New York: LearningExpress, 1997.
———*Firefighter Exam New York*. New York: LearningExpress, 1997.
———*Firefighter Exam New York City*. New York: LearningExpress, 1998.
———*Firefighter Exam the South*. New York: LearningExpress, 1997.
———*Firefighter Exam Texas*. New York: LearningExpress, 1997.
———*The Secrets of Taking Any Test*. New York: LearningExpress, 2000.
LearningExpress Website
www.learnatest.com

SKILL BUILDERS

LearningExpress. *Algebra Success*. New York: LearningExpress, 2000.
———*Geometry Success*. New York: LearningExpress, 2000.
———*Math Essentials*. New York: LearningExpress, 2000.
———*Practical Math Success*. New York: LearningExpress, 1998.
———*Reasoning Skills Success*. New York: LearningExpress, 1998.

———*Vocabulary & Spelling Success*. New York: LearningExpress, 1998.

———*501 Challenging Logic & Reasoning Problems*. New York: LearningExpress, 1999.

———*501 Reading Comprehension Questions*. New York: LearningExpress, 1999.

———*1001 Math Problems*. New York: LearningExpress, 1999.

———*1001 Vocabulary & Spelling Questions*. New York: LearningExpress, 1999.

Appendix D

Directory of Fire-Related Training Programs

This section provides a listing of schools in each state that offer fire-related training programs. These programs offer a range of training choices—from certificate to associate and bachelor's degrees—and include fire science, fire technology, fire protection engineering, fire administration, and fire protection technology programs. The schools are listed in alphabetical order by city in each state, so you can quickly locate schools that are near you. All programs provide school name, address, and phone number, so you can contact them directly to get more information and application forms.

This listing is intended to help you begin your search for an appropriate school. The schools included in this listing, however, are not endorsed or recommended by LearningExpress. We have not included every school that offers fire science programs in every state, so we recommend that you use this list as a starting point but that you do further research to see if there are other schools that you might like to consider.

Always contact the schools you are considering to get current information on program requirements and areas of specialization before you apply. And remember that information provided here may change; use the Internet and college guides to find out more about these schools, and to find others that may offer the program(s) you are interested in.

ALABAMA

Jefferson State Community College
2601 Carson Road
Birmingham, AL 35215-3098
205-853-1200
Website: www.jscc.cc.al.us

Lawson State Community College
3060 Wilson Road SW
Birmingham, AL 35221-1798
205-925-2515
Website: www.ls.cc.al.us

Wallace State Community College
P.O. Box 2000
Hanceville, AL 35077-2000
256-352-8337
Website: www.wallace.edu

Community College of the Air Force
Maxwell Air Force Base, AL 36112-6613
334-953-6436
Website: www.au.af.mil

Northwest-Shoals Community College
P.O. Box 2545
Muscle Shoals, AL 35662
256-331-6218
Website: http://nwscc.cc.al.us

Northwest Alabama Community College
Route 3, Box 77
Phil Campbell, AL 35581
205-993-5331
Website: www.nwscc.cc.al.us

Chattahoochee Valley State Community
College
119 Broad Street
Phoenix City, AL 36969-7928
334-291-4928
Website: www.cvcc.cc.al.us

George Corley Wallace State Community
College
3000 Earl Goodwin Parkway
Selma, AL 36702-1049
334-876-9227
Website: http://wccs.cc.al.us

Shelton State Community College/Alabama
Fire College
1301 15th Street East
Tuscaloosa, AL 35404
205-759-1541
-or-
205-391-3744
Website: www.alabamafirecollege.cc.al.us

Southern Union State Community College
Roberts Street
Wadley, AL 36276
256-395-2211
Website: www.suscc.cc.al.us

ALASKA

Community and Technical College
University of Alaska
3211 Providence Drive
Anchorage, AK 99508-8306
907-786-6400
Website: www.uaa.alaska.edu/ctc

University of Alaska
Tanana Valley Campus
510 Second Avenue
Fairbanks, AK 99701
907-474-7400
Website: www.alaska.edu

University of Alaska Anchorage
Matanuska-Susitna College
P.O. Box 2889
Palmer, AK 99645-2889
907-745-9726
Website: www.uaa.alaska.edu

ARIZONA
Cochise College
Douglas, AZ 85607-9724
520-515-0500
Website: www.conchise.cc.as.us

Coconino County Community College
3000 North 4th Street
Flagstaff, AZ 86003
520-527-1222
Website: www.coco.cc.ac.us

Glendale Community College
6000 West Olive Avenue
Glendale, AZ 85302-3090
623-845-3000
Website: www.gc.maricopa.edu

Northland Pioneer College
203 West Hopi Drive
Holbrook, AZ 86025-0610
520-524-1993
Website: www.northland.cc.az.us

Estrella Mountain Community College
3000 North Dysart Road
Litchfield Park, AZ 85340
623-935-8000
Website: www.emc.maricopa.edu

Mohave Community College
1971 Jagerson Avenue
Kingman, AZ 86401-1299
520-757-0847
Website: www.mohave.cc.az.us/mcchome.
    html

Mesa Community College
1833 West Southern Avenue
Mesa, AZ 85202-4866
480-461-7000
Website: www.mc.maricopa.edu

Phoenix College
1202 West Thomas Road
Phoenix, AZ 85013-4234
602-285-7500
Website: www.maricopa.edu

Rio Salado Community College
640 North 1st Avenue
Phoenix, AZ 85003
480-517-8000
Website: www.rio.maricopa.edu

Yavapai College
1100 East Sheldon Street
Prescott, AZ 86301-3297
520-776-2158
Website: www.yavapai.cc.az.us

Scottsdale Community College
9000 East Chaparral Road
Scottsdale, AZ 85250-2699
480-423-6100
Website: www.sc.maricopa.edu

Cochise College-Sierra Vista Campus
901 North Colombo
Sierra Vista, AZ 85635-2317
520-515-5412
Website: www.cochise.org

Pima County Community College
2202 West Anklam Road
Tucson, AZ 85706
520-206-7000
Website: www.pima.edu

Arizona Western College
9500 S. Avenue 8E
Yuma, AZ 85365
520-317-6000
Website: www.awc.cc.az.us

ARKANSAS
SAU Tech Station
100 Carr Road
Camden, AK 71701
870-574-4500
Website: www.sautech.edu

Cossatot Technical College
P.O. Box 960
DeQueen, AK 71832
870-584-4471
Website: http://cossatot.ctc.tec.ar.us

Garland County Community College
101 College Drive
Hot Springs, AK 71913-9174
501-760-4155
Website: www.gccc.cc.ar.us

Black River Technical College
1416 Highway 304 East
Pocahontas, AK 72455
870-892-4565
Website: www.brtc.tec.ar.us

CALIFORNIA
Cabrillo College
6500 Soquel Drive
Aptos, CA 95003-3194
831-479-6201
Website: www.cabrillo.cc.ca.us

Bakersfield College
1801 Panorama Drive
Bakersfield, CA 93305-1299
661-395-4301
Website: www.bc.cc.ca.us

University of California
Fire Safety Engineering Science
Davis Hall
Berkeley, CA 94720
510-643-8415
Website: www.ucop.edu

Palo Verde College
811 West Chanslor Way
Blythe, CA 92225-1118
760-922-6168
Website: www.paloverde.cc.ca.us

Southwestern College
900 Otay Lakes Road
Chula Vista, CA 91910
619-421-6700
Website: www.swc.cc.ca.us

Columbia College
11600 Columbia College Drive
Sonora, CA 95370
209-588-5100
Website: www.columbiayosemite.cc.ca.us

Compton Community College
1111 East Artesia Blvd.
Compton, CA 90221-5393
310-637-2660
Website: www.compton.cc.ca.us

Fresno City College
1101 East University Avenue
Fresno, CA 93741-0002
559-442-4600
Website: www.fcc.cc.ca.us

Glendale Community College
1500 North Verdugo Road
Glendale, CA 91208-2894
818-240-1000
Website: www.glendale.cc.ca.us

Chabot College
25555 Hesperian Blvd.
Hayward, CA 94545-5001
510-723-6700
Website: www.clpccd.cc.ca.us

Imperial Valley College
380 East Aten Road
P.O. Box 158
Highway 111 and Aten Road
Imperial, CA 92251-0158
760-352-8320
Website: www.imperial.cc.ca.us

Copper Mountain College
P.O. Box 1398
Joshua Tree, CA 92252
760-366-3791

College of Marin
835 College Avenue
Kentfield, CA 94904
415-457-8811
Website: www.marin.cc.ca.us

Antelope Valley College
3041 W. Avenue K
Lancaster, CA 93536
666-722-6300
Website: www.avc.edu

Las Positas College
3033 Collier Canyon Road
Livermore, CA 94550-7650
925-373-5800
Website: www.laspositas.cc.ca.us

Long Beach City College
4901 East Carson Street
Long Beach, CA 90808-1780
562-938-4111
Website: www.lbcc.cc.ca.us

California State University
Department of Industrial Studies
5151 University Drive
Los Angeles, CA 90032-8530
323-343-3000
Website: www.calstatela.edu

Yuba College
2088 North Beale Road
Marysville, CA 95901-7699
530-741-6700
Website: www.yuba.cc.ca.us

Merced College
3600 M Street
Merced, CA 95348-2898
209-384-6190
Website: www.merced.cc.ca.us

Modesto Junior College
435 College Avenue
Modesto, CA 95350-5800
209-549-7028
Website: http://gomjc.org

East Los Angeles College
1301 Avenida Cesaer Chavez
Monterey Park, CA 91754-6001
323-265-8650
Website: www.elac.cc.ca.us

Monterey Peninsula College
980 Fremont Street
Monterey, CA 93940-4799
831-646-4006
Website: www.mpc.edu

Merritt College
12500 Campus Drive
Oakland, CA 94619-3196
510-436-2598
Website: www.peralta.cc.ca.us

Butte Community College
3536 Butte Campus Drive
Oroville, CA 95965-8399
530-895-2511
Website: www.cin.butte.cc.ca.us

Oxnard College
4000 South Rose Avenue
Oxnard, CA 93033-6699
805-488-0911
Website: www.oxnard.cc.ca.us

College of the Desert
43500 Monterey Avenue
Palm Desert, CA 92260-9305
760-773-2519
Website: www.desert.cc.ca.us

Pasadena City College
1570 East Colorado Blvd.
Pasadena, CA 91106
626-585-7123
Website: www.paccd.cc.ca.us

Los Medanos College
2700 East Leland Road
Pittsburg, CA 94565-5197
925-429-2181
Website: www.losmedanos.net

Porterville College
100 East College Avenue
Porterville, CA 93257-6058
559-791-2200
Website: www.pc.cc.ca.us

Shasta College
P.O. Box 496006
Redding, CA 96049-6006
530-225-4769
Website: www.shastacollege.edu

Riverside Community College
4800 Magnolia Avenue
Riverside, CA 92506-1293
909-222-8615
Website: www.rccd.cc.ca.us

Sierra Community College
5000 Rocklin Road
Rocklin, CA 95677-3397
916-781-0430
Website: www.sierra.cc.ca.us

American River College
4700 College Oak Drive
Sacramento, CA 95841-4286
916-484-8261
Website: www.arc.losrios.cc.ca.us

Cosumnes River College
8401 Center Parkway
Sacramento, CA 95823-5799
916-688-7410
Website: www.crc.losrios.cc.ca.us

San Diego Miramar College
10440 Black Mountain Road
San Diego, CA 92126-2999
858-536-7800
Website: www.miramarcollege.net

City College of San Francisco
50 Phelan Avenue
San Francisco, CA 94112-1821
415-239-3000
Website: www.ccsf.cc.ca.us

Mount San Jacinto College
21400 Highway 79
San Jacinto, CA 92383-2399
909-487-6752
Website: www.msjc.cc.ca.us

Palomar Community College
1140 West Mission Road
San Marcos, CA 92069-1487
760-744-1150
Website: www.palomar.edu

College of San Mateo
1700 West Hillsdale Blvd.
San Mateo, CA 94402-3784
650-574-6161
Website: www.gocsm.net

Santa Anna College
1530 West 17th Street
Santa Anna, CA 92706-3398
714-564-6000
Website: www.sacollege.org

Mission College
3000 Mission College Blvd.
Santa Clara, CA 95054-1897
408-748-2700
Website: www.mvmccd.cc.ca.us/mc

Allan Hancock College
800 South College Drive
Santa Maria, CA 93454-6399
805-922-6966
Website: www.hancock.cc.ca.us

Santa Monica College
1900 Pico Blvd.
Santa Monica, CA 90405-1644
310-434-4000
Website: www.smc.edu

Santa Rosa Junior College
1501 Mendocino Avenue
Santa Rosa, CA 95401-4395
707-527-4011
Website: www.santarosa.edu

Columbia College
11600 Columbia College Drive
Sonora, CA 95370
209-588-5231
Website: http://gocolumbia.org

Lake Tahoe Community College
One College Drive
South Lake Tahoe, CA 96150-4524
530-541-4660
Website: www.ltcc.cc.ca.us

San Joaquin Delta Community College
5151 Pacific Avenue
Stockton, CA 95207-6370
209-954-5151
Website: www.deltacollege.org

Solano Community College
P.O. Box 246
Suisun City, CA 94585-3197
707-864-7171
Website: www.solano.cc.ca.us

Cogswell Polytechnical College
1175 Bordeaux Drive
Sunnyville, CA 94089-1299
408-541-0100
Website: www.cogswell.edu

El Camino College
16007 Crenshaw Blvd.
Torrance, CA 90506-0001
310-660-3414
Website: www.elcamino.cc.ca.us

Los Angeles Valley College
5800 Fulton Avenue
Van Nuys, CA 91401-4096
818-781-1200
Website: www.lavc.cc.ca.us

Victor Valley Community College
18422 Bear Valley Road
Victorville, CA 92392-5849
760-245-4271
Website: www.vvcconline.com

College of Sequoias
915 South Mooney Blvd.
Visalia, CA 93277-2234
559-730-3700
Website: www.sequoias.cc.ca.us

Mt. San Antonio College
1100 North Grand Avenue
Walnut, CA 91789-1399
909-594-5611
Website: http://zeus.mtsac.edu

College of the Siskiyous
800 College Avenue
Weed, CA 96094-2899
530-938-5215
Website: www.siskiyous.edu

Rio Hondo College
3600 Workman Mill Road
Whittier, CA 90601-1699
562-692-0921
Website: www.rh.cc.ca.us

Los Angeles Harbor College
1111 South Figueroa Place
Wilmington, CA 90744-2311
310-522-8214
Website: www.lahc.cc.ca.us

Crafton Hills College
11711 Sand Canyon Road
Yucaipa, CA 92399-1799
909-389-3372
Website: www.sbccd.cc.ca.us/chc

COLORADO

Community College of Aurora
16000 East Centretech Parkway
Aurora, CO 80011
303-360-4792
Website: www.cca.ccc.oes.edu

Pikes Peak Community College
5675 South Academy Blvd.
Colorado Springs, CO 80906-5498
719-540-7650
Website: www.ppcc.cccoes.edu

Colorado Mountain College
Summit Campus
Breckenridge Center
103 S. Harris Street
P.O. Box 2208
Breckenridge, CO 80424
970-453-6757
Website:www.coloradomtn.edu/campus_sum/
 home

Colorado Mountain College
Vail/Eagle Valley Campus
139 Broadway
P.O. Box 249
Eagle, CO 81631
970-328-6304
Website:www.coloradomtn.edu/campus_
    vev/home

Aims Community College
P.O. Box 69
Greeley, CO 80632-0069
970-330-8008
Website: www.aims.edu

Red Rocks Community College
13300 West 6th Avenue
Lakewood, CO 80228-1255
303-988-6160
Website: www.rrcc.cccoes.edu

Arapahoe Community College
2500 West College Drive
P.O. Box 9002
Littleton, CO 80160-9002
303-797-5900
Website: www.arapahoe.edu

CONNECTICUT

Capital Community College
61 Woodland Street
Hartford, CT 06105
860-520-7800

Gateway Community Technical College
60 Sargent Drive
New Haven, CT 06511
203-285-2010
Website: www.online.commnet.edu

Charter Oak State College
55 Paul Manafort Drive
New Britain, CT 06053
860-832-3800
Website: www.cocs.edu

Norwalk State Technical College
188 Richards Avenue
Norwalk, CT 06854-1655
203-857-7060
Website: www.ncc.commnet.edu

Three Rivers Community College
547 New London Turnpike
Norwich, CT 06360
860-823-2860
Website: www.trctc.commnet.edu

Naugatuack Valley Community Technical
College
750 Chase Parkway
Waterbury, CT 06708-3000
203-575-8078
Website: www.nvcc.commnet.edu

University of New Haven
Fire Science Department
300 Orange Avenue
West Haven, CT 06516-1916
203-932-7088
Website: www.newhaven.edu

DELAWARE
Delaware Technical & Community College
Stanton Campus
400 Stanton Christiana Road
Newark, NJ 19713
302-454-3954
Website: www.dtcc.edu

DISTRICT OF COLUMBIA
University of the District of Columbia
4200 Connecticut Avenue
NW Washington, DC 20008-1175
202-274-5000
Website: www.udc.edu

FLORIDA
Manatee Community College
Brandenton Campus
5840 26th Street West
Brandenton, FL 34207-1849
941-752-5000
Website: www.mcc.cc.fl.us

Brevard Community College
1519 Clear Lake Road
Cocoa, FL 32922-6597
321-632-1111
Website: www.brevard.cc.fl.us

Pasco-Hernando Community College
36727 Blanton Road
Dade City, FL 33523-7599
352-567-6701
Website: www.pasco-hernandocc.com

Wm. T. McFatter Vocational Tech Center
6500 Nova Drive
Davie, FL 33317
954-474-8217
Website: www.mcfattertech.com

Daytona Beach Community College
Daytona Beach, FL 32120
904-254-4426
Website: www.dbcc.cc.fl.us

Broward Community College
225 East Las Olas Blvd.
Fort Lauderdale, FL 33301-2298
954-761-7464
Website: www.broward.cc.fl.us

Edison Community College
8099 College Parkway S.W.
Fort Meyers, FL 33906-6210
941-489-9361
Website: www.edison.edu

Indian River Community College
3209 Virginia Avenue
Fort Pierce, FL 34981
561-462-4740
Website: www.ircc.cc.fl.us

Florida Community College at Jacksonville
501 West State Street
Jacksonville, FL 32202-4030
904-646.2300
Website: www.fccj.cc.fl.us

Palm Beach Junior College
4200 Congress Avenue
Lake Worth, FL 33461-4796
561-967-7222
Website: www.pbcc.cc.fl.us

Lake-Sumter Community College
Leesburg Campus
9501 U.S. Highway 441
Leesburg, FL 34788-8751
352-787-3747
Website: www.lscc.cc.fl.us

Chipola Junior College
3094 Indian Circle
Marianna, FL 32446-2053
850-526-2761
Website: www.chipola.cc.fl.us

Miami Dade Community College
300 N.E. Second Avenue
Miami, FL 33132-2296
305-237-7478
Website: www.mdcc.edu

James Lorenzo Walker Vocational
3702 Estey Avenue
Naples, FL 33942-4457
941-434-4815
Website: www.collier.k12.fl.us

Central Florida Community College
P.O. Box 1388
Ocala, FL 34478-1388
352-237-2111
Website: www.cfcc.cc.fl.us

Florida State Fire College
11655 NW Gainesville Road
Ocala, FL 34482-1486
352-732-1330
Website: www.fsfc.ufl.edu

Valencia Community College
P.O. Box, FL 3028
Orlando, FL 32802-3028
407-299-5000
Website: www.valencia.cc.fl.us

St. Johns River Community College
5001 St. Johns Avenue
Palatka, FL 32177-3807
904-312-4200
Website: www.sjrcc.cc.fl.us

Gulf Coast Community College
5230 West Highway 98
Panama City, FL 32401-1058
850-769-1551
Website: www.gc.cc.cc.fl.us

Naval Air Technical Training Center
Naval Air Station Pensacola
230 Chevalier Field Avenue
Pensacola, FL 32508-5113
904-452-7212
Website: www.cnet.navy.mil/cnet/nattc

Pensacola Junior College
1000 College Boulevard
Pensacola, FL 32504-8998
850-484-1000
Website: www.pjc.cc.fl.us

St. Augustine Tech Center
2980 Collins Avenue
St. Augustine, FL 32095-9970
904-824-4401
Website: www.fcti.org

St. Petersburg Junior College
P.O. Box 13489
St. Petersburg, FL 33733-3489
727-341-3239
Website: www.spjc.cc.fl.us

Pinellas Technical Education Center
St. Petersburg Campus
901 34th Street South
St. Petersburg, FL 33711
727-893-2500
Website: www.ptecclw.pinellas.k12.fl.us

Seminole Community College
Highway 17-29
Sanford, FL 32773-6199
407-328-2025
Website: www.scc.-fl.com

Sarasota County Technical Institute
4748 Beneva Road
Sarasota, FL 34233
941-924-1365
Website: www.careerscape.org

Hillsborough Community College
P.O. Box, FL 31127
Tampa, FL 33631
813-253-7004
Website: www.hcc.cc.fl.us

Polk Community College
999 Avenue "H" N.E.
Winter Haven, FL 33881-4299
863-297-1009
Website: www.polk.cc.fl.us

Ridge Technical Center
7700 State Road 544
Winter Haven, FL 33881
863-299-2512
Website: www.pcsb.k12.fl.us

GEORGIA
Dekalb Community College
555 North Indian Creek Road
Clarkston, GA 30021-2396
404-299-4564
Website: www.gpc.peachnet.edu

Macon State College
100 College Station Drive
Macon, GA 31206
478-471-2700
Website: www.maconstate.edu

Savannah Technical Institute
5717 White Bluff Road
Savannah, GA 31499
912-351-6362
Website: www.savannah.tec.ga.us

HAWAII

Honolulu Community College

874 Dillingham Blvd.

Honolulu, HI 96817-4598

808-845-9129

Website: www.hcc.hawaii.edu

IDAHO

Boise State University

College of Technology

1910 University Drive

Boise, ID 83725

208-426-1011

Website: www.idbsu.edu

Eastern Idaho Tech College

25th East

Idaho Falls, ID 83404-5788

208-524-3000

Website: www.eitc.edu

Lewis-Clark State College

School of Technology

500 8th Avenue

Lewiston, ID 83501-2698

208-799-5272

Website: www.lcsc.edu

Idaho State University

Fire Service Technology

P.O. Box 8054

Pocatello, ID 82309

208-236-2123

Website: www.isu.edu

College of Southern Idaho

315 Falls Avenue

P.O. Box 1238

Twin Falls, ID 83303-1238

208-733-9554

Website: www.csi.cc.id.us

ILLINOIS

Southwestern Illinois College

2500 Carlyle Avenue

Belleville, IL 62221-5899

618-235-2700

Website: www.southwestern.cc.il.us

Spoon River College

23235 North County 22

Canton, IL 61520

309-647-4645

Website: www.spoonrivercollege.net

Southern Illinois University

Carbondale Campus

Carbondale, IL 62901-6806

618-536-4405

Website: www.siu.edu

Parkland College

2400 West Bradley Avenue

Champaign, IL 61821-1899

217-351-2482

Website: www.parkland.cc.il.us

City Colleges of Chicago
Harold Washington College
30 East Lake Street
Chicago, IL 60601
312-553-6000
Website: www.ccc.edu/hwashington

Prairie State College
202 South Halstead Street
Chicago Heights, IL 60411-8226
708-709-3516
Website: www.prairie.cc.il.us

McHenry County College
8900 U.S. Highway 14
Crystal Lake, IL 60012-2761
815-455-8716
Website: www.mchenry.cc.il.us

Richland Community College
One College Park
Decatur, IL 62521
217-875-7200
Website: www.richland.cc.il.us

Oakton Community College
1600 East Gulf
Des Plaines, IL 60016-1268
847-635-1703
Website: www.oakton.edu

Illinois Central College
One College Drive
East Peoria, IL 61635-0001
309-694-5235
Website: www.icc.cc.il.us

Elgin Community College
1700 Spartan Drive
Elgin, IL 60123-7193
847-888-7385
Website: www.elgin.cc.il.us

College of DuPage
425 22nd St.
Glen Ellyn, IL 60137
630-858-2800
Website: www.cod.edu

Lewis and Clark Community College
5800 Godfrey Road
Godfrey, IL 62035-2466
618-466-3411
Website: www.lc.cc.il.us

College of Lake County
19351 W. Washington Street
Grayslake, IL 60030
847-223-6601
Website: www.clc.cc.il.us

Southeastern Illinois College
3575 College Road
Harrisburg, IL 62946
618-252-6376
Website: www.sic.cc.il.us

Joliet Junior College
1215 Houbolt Road
Joliet, IL 60431-8938
815-729-9020
Website: www.jjc.cc.il.us

Kishwaukee College
21193 Malta Road
Malta, IL 60150
815-825-2086
Website: www.kish.cc.il.us

Illinois Valley Community College
815 North Orlando Smith Avenue
Oglesby, IL 61348-9691
815-224-2720
Website: www.ivcc.edu

William Rainey Harper College
1200 West Algonquin Road
Palatine, IL 60067
847-925-6000
Website: www.harpercollege.com

Moraine Valley Community College
10900 South 88th Avenue
Palos Hills, IL 60465
708-974-4300
Website: www.moraine.cc.il.us

John Wood Community College
150 South 48th Street
Quincy, IL 62301
217-224-6500
Website: www.jwcc.edu

Triton College
2000 Fifth Avenue
River Grove, IL 60171
708-456-0300
Website: www.triton.cc.il.us

Rock Valley College
3301 North Mulford Road
Rockford, IL 61114-5699
815-654-4286
Website: www.rvc.cc.il.us

South Suburban College
15800 South State Street
South Holland, IL 60473
708-596-2000
Website: www.ssc.cc.il.us

Lincoln Land Community College
5250 Shepard Road
P.O. Box 19256
Springfield, IL 62794-9256
800-727-4161
Website: www.llcc.cc.il.us

Waubonsee Community College
Route 47 at Waubonsee Drive
Sugar Grove, IL 60554
630-466-7900
Website: www.wcc.cc.il.us

INDIANA
Ivy Tech State College
Northeast Indiana
3800 North Anthony Blvd.
Fort Wayne, IN 46805-1430
219-480-4211
Website: www.ivy.tec.in.us/fortwayne

Ivy Tech State College Northwest
Northwest Indiana
1440 East 35th Avenue
Gary, IN 46409-1479
219-981-1111
Website: www.gar.ivy.tec.in.us

Ivy Tech State College
Central Indiana
One West 26th Street
Indianapolis, IN 46208
317-921-4800
Website: www.ivytec.in.us/indianapolis

IOWA

Fire Service Training Bureau
Division of State Fire Marshall
3100 Fire Service Road
Ames, IA 50011-3100
515-294-6817
Website: www.state.ia.us/government/
    dps/fm/fstb

Des Moines Area Community College
2006 Ankeny Blvd.
Ankeny, IA 50021
515-964-6210
Website: www.dmacc.org

Kirkwood Community College
6301 Kirkwood Blvd., SW
P.O. Box 2068
Cedar Rapids, IA 52406-2068
319-398-5517
Website: www.kirkwood.cc.ia.us

Iowa Western Community College
2700 College Road, Box 4-C
Council Bluffs, IA 51502
712-325-3200
Website: www.iwcc.cc.ia.us

Western Iowa Technical Community College
4647 Stone Avenue
PO 5199
Sioux City, IA 51106
712-274-6400
Website: www.witcc.cc.ia.us

KANSAS

Dodge City Community Junior College
2501 North 14th Avenue
Dodge City, KS 67801-2399
316-225-1321
Website: www.dccc.cc.ks.us

Butler County Community College
901 South Haverill Road
El Dorado, KS 67042-3280
316-321-2222
Website: www.buccc.cc.ks.us

Barton County Community College
245 NE 30th Road
Great Bend, KS 67530-9283
316-792-2701
Website: www.barton.cc.ks.us

Hutchinson Community Junior College
1300 North Plum
Hutchinson, KS 67501-5894
316-665-3536
Website: www.hutchcc.edu

Kansas City Kansas Community College
7250 State Avenue
Kansas City, KS 66112-3003
913-334-1100
Website: www.kckcc.cc.kc.us

Johnson County Community College
12345 College Blvd. at Quivira
Overland Park, KS 66210-1299
913-469-8500
Website: www.jccc.ks.net

Labette Community College
200 South 14th
Parsons, KS 67357-4299
316-421-6700
Website: www.labette.cc.ks.us

KENTUCKY

Jefferson Community College
109 East Broadway
Louisville, KY 40202-2005
502-584-0181
Website: www.jcc.uky.edu

Eastern Kentucky University
College of Law Enforcement
Richmond, KY 40475-3101
859-622-2106
Website: www.eku.edu

LOUISIANA

Louisiana State University
Division of Continuing Education
Baton Rouge, LA 70803
225-388-1686
Website: www.lsu.edu

Louisiana State University at Eunice
P.O. Box 1129
Eunice, LA 70535-1129
337-457-7311
Website: www.lsue.edu

Delgado College
615 City Park Avenue
New Orleans, LA 70119-4399
504-483-4004
Website: www.dcc.edu

MAINE

Southern Maine Technical College
2 Fort Road
South Portland, ME 04106
207-767-9520
Website: www.smtc.net

MARYLAND

Catonsville Community College
800 South Rolling Road
Catonsville, MD 21228-5381
410-455-4304
Website: www.ccbc.cc.md.us

University of Maryland
Dept. of Fire Protection Engineering
College Park, MD 20472
301-314-8385
Website: www.uga.umd.edu

Montgomery College
51 Manakee Street
Rockville, MD 20850-1196
301-279-5034
Website: www.montgomerycollege.org

MASSACHUSETTS

Middlesex Community College
591 Springs Road
Bedford, MA 01730-1197
800-818-3434
Website: www.middlesex.cc.ma.us

Bunker Hill Community College
250 New Rutherford Avenue
Boston, MA 02129-2991
617-228-2000
Website: www.bhcc.state.ma.us

Massasoit Community College
290 Thatcher Street
Brockton, MA 02402-3996
508-588-9100
Website: www.massasoit.ma.edu

North Shore Community College
1 Ferncroft Road
Danvers, MA 01923-4093
978-762-4000
Website: www.nscc.mass.edu

Bristol Community College
777 Elsbree Street
Fall River, MA 02720-7395
508-678-2811
Website: www.bristol.mass.edu

Mount Wachusett Community College
444 Green Street
Gardner, MA 01440-1000
978-632-6600 ext. 110
Website: www.mwcc.mass.edu

Greenfield Community College
1 College Drive
Greenfield, MA 01301
413-774-3131
Website: www.gcc.mass.edu

Northeast Maritime, Inc.
66 Spring Street
New Bedford, MA 02740
508-992-4025
Website: www.northeastmaritime.com

Anna Maria College
50 Sunset Lane
Paxton, MA 01612-1198
508-849-3300
Website: www.annamaria.edu

Berkshire Community College
1350 West Street
Pittsfield, MA 01201-5786
413-499-4660
Website: http://cc.berkshire.org

Quincy College
34 Coddington Street
Quincy, MA 02169-4522
617-984-1700
Website: www.quincycollege.com

Salem State College
352 Lafayette Street
Salem, MA 01970
978-542-6000
Website: www.salem.mass.edu

Springfield Technical Community College
1 Armory Square
Springfield, MA 01105-1296
413-781-7822
Website: www.stcc.mass.edu

Massachusetts Bay Community College
50 Oakland Street
Wellesley Hills, MA 02481
781-239-3000
Website: www.mbcc.mass.edu

Cape Cod Community College
2240 Iyanough Road
West Barnstable, MA 02668-1599
508-362-2131
Website: www.capecod.mass.edu

Quinsigamond Community College
670 West Boylston Street
Worcester, MA 01606-2092
508-853-2300
Website: www.qcc.mass.edu

Worcester Polytechnic Institute
Center for Fire Safety Studies
100 Institute Road
Worcester, MA 01609-2280
508-831-5286
Website: www.wpi.edu

MICHIGAN

Washtenaw Community College
4800 E. Huron River Drive
P.O. Box D-1
Ann Arbor, MI 48106
734-973-3300
Website: www.washtenaw.cc.mi.us

Oakland Community College
Auburn Hills Campus
2900 Featherstone Road
Auburn Hills, MI 48326-2845
248-232-4100
Website: www.occ.cc.mi.us

Kellogg Community College
450 North Avenue
Battle Creek, MI 49017-3397
616-965-3931
Website: www.kellogg.cc.mi.us

Glen Oaks Community College
62249 Shimmel Road
Centreville, MI 49032-9719
616-467-9945
Website: www.glenoaks.cc.mi.us

Henry Ford Community College
5101 Evergreen Road
Dearborn, MI 48128
313-845-9600
Website: www.henryford.cc.mi.us

Southwestern Michigan College
58900 Cherry Grove Road
Dowagiac, MI 49047-9793
616-782-1000
Website: www.smc.cc.mi.us

Mott Community College
1401 East Court Street
Flint, MI 48503-2089
810-762-0200
Website: www.program.mcc.edu/fire_
    protection_technology

Mid-Michigan Community College
1375 South Clare Avenue
Harrison, MI 48625-9447
517-386-6622
Website: www.midmich.cc.mi.us

Kalamazoo Valley Community College
P.O. Box, MI 4070
Kalamazoo, MI 49003-4070
616-372-5000
Website: www.kvcc.edu

Lansing Community College
419 North Capitol Avenue
Lansing, MI 48901-7210
517-483-1957
Website: www.lansing.cc.mi.us

Madonna University
36600 Schoolcraft Road
Livonia, MI 48150-1173
734-432-4951
Website: www.munet.edu

Schoolcraft College
18600 Haggerty Road
Livonia, MI 48152-2696
734-462-4426
Website: www.schoolcraft.cc.mi.us

Macomb Community College
Center Campus
44575 Garfield Road
Clinton Township, MI 48038-1139
810-286-2228
Website: www.macomb.cc.mi.us

St. Clair County Community College
323 Erie Street
Port Huron, MI 48061-5015
810-989-5500
Website: www.stclair.cc.mi.us

Lake Superior State University
650 West Easterday Avenue
Sault Saint Marie, MI 49783
906-635-2231
Website: www.lssu.edu

Macomb Community College
14500 Twelve Mile Road
Box 309
Warren, MI 48093-3896
810-445-7211
Website: www.macomb.cc.mi.us

Delta College
Admissions Office
University Center, MI 48710
517-686-9092
Website: www.delta.edu

MINNESOTA

Lake Superior College
2101 Trinity Road
Duluth 55811
218-733-7600
Website: www.lsc.cc.mn.us

Northwest Technical College
2022 Central Avenue N.E.
East Grand Forks, MN 56721-2702
218-773-3441
Website: www.ntc-online.com

Hennepin Technical College
9200 Flying Cloud Drive
Eden Prairie, MN 56347
612-550-3112
Website: www.htc.mnscu.edu

North Hennepin Community College
7411 85th Avenue North
Minneapolis, MN 55445
612-425-3800
Website: www.nh.cc.mn.us

MISSISSIPPI

Mississippi Gulf Coast Community College
Jefferson Davis Campus
2226 Switzer Road
Gulfport, MS 39507
228-896-2500
Website: www.mgccc.cc.ms.us

Meridian Community College
910 Highway 19 North
Meridian, MS 39307
601-484-8622
Website: www.mcc.cc.ms.us

East Mississippi Community College
P.O. Box 158
Scooba, MS 39358-0158
662-476-8442
Website: www.emcc.cc.ms.us

MISSOURI

University of Missouri
Center for Independent Study
136 Clark Hall
Columbia, MO 65211
573-882-7786
Website: www.missouri.edu

Jefferson College
Hillsboro, MO 63050-2441
636-789-3951

Penn Valley Community College
3201 Southwest Trafficway
Kansas City, MO 64111
816-759-4101
Website: www.kcmetro.cc.mo.us

Crowder College
601 Laclede Avenue
Neosho, MO 64850-9160
417-451-3223
Website: www.crowder.cc.mo.us

Ozarks Technical Community College
P.O. Box 5958
Springfield, MO 65801
417-895-7000
Website: www.otc.cc.mo.us

St. Louis Community College
at Florissant Valley
3400 Pershall Road
St. Louis, MO 63135-1499
314-595-4200
Website: www.stlcc.cc.mo.us

St. Louis Community College
at Forest Park
5600 Oakland Avenue
St. Louis, MO 63110-1316
314-644-9100
Website: www.stlcc.cc.mo.us/fp

East Central Missouri Junior College
P.O. Box 529
Union, MO 63084-0529
636-583-5195
Website: www.ecc.cc.mo.us

Central Missouri State University
School of Public Service
Warrensburg, MO 64093
800-729-2678

MONTANA

Montana State University
College of Technology-Great Falls
2100 16th Avenue South
Great Falls, MT 59405
406-771-4312
Website: www.msugs.edu

Helena College of Technology
of the University of Montana
Helena, MT 59601
406-444-6800
Website: www.hct.umontana.edu

Miles Community College
2715 Dickinson Street
Miles City, MT 59301-4799
800-541-9281
Website: www.mcc.cc.mt.us

NEBRASKA

Southeast Community College

Lincoln Campus

8800 "O" Street

Lincoln, NE 68520-1299

402-471-3333

Website: www.college.sccm.cc.ne.us

University of Nebraska-Lincoln

Office of Admissions

Alexander Building

1410 Q Street

P.O. Box 880417

Lincoln, NE 68588-0417

402-472-2023

Website: www.unl.edu

Mid-Plains Technical Community College

Interstate 20 and Highway 83

North Platte, NE 69101-9491

308-532-8740

Website: www.mpcc.ne.us

University of Nebraska at Omaha

Alexander Building

College of Engineering

P.O. Box, NE 688

Omaha, NE 68182

402-554-2800

Website: www.unomaha.edu

NEVADA

Western Nevada Community College

2201 West College Parkway

Carson City, NV 89703

772-445-3000

Great Basin College

1500 College Parkway

Elko, NV 89801

775-738-8493

Website: www.gbcnv.edu

Community College of Southern Nevada

Cheyenne Campus

3200 East Cheyenne Avenue

North Las Vegas, NV 89030-4296

702-651-3038

Website: www.ccsn.nevada.edu

Truckee Meadows Community College

7000 Dandini Blvd.

Reno, NV 89512-3901

775-673-7000

Website: www.tmcc.edu/fireacademy

NEW HAMPSHIRE

New Hampshire Community Technical

College

379 New Prescott Hill Road

Laconia, NH 03246

603-524-3207

Website: www.laco.tec.nh.us

NEW JERSEY

Camden County College

P.O. Box 200

Blackwood, NJ 08012-0200

856-227-7200

Website: www.camdencc.edu

Union County College
1033 Springfield Avenue
Cranford, NJ 07016-1528
908-709-7000
Website: www.ucc.edu

Middlesex County College
2600 Woodbridge Avenue
P.O. Box 3050
Edison, NJ 08818-3050
732-548-6000
Website: www.middlesex.cc.nj.us

Jersey City State College
2039 Kennedy Blvd.
Jersey City, NJ 07305-1597
201-200-2000
Website: www.jcstate.edu

Brookdale Community College
765 Newman Springs Road
Lincroft, NJ 07738-1597
732-224-2375
Website: www.brookdale.cc.nj.us

Essex County College
303 University Avenue
Newark, NJ 07102-1798
973-877-3000
Website: www.essex.edu

Sussex Community College
One College Hill
Newton, NJ 07860
973-300-2100
Website: www.sussex.cc.nj.us

Passaic County Community College
One College Blvd.
Patterson, NJ 07505-1179
973-684-6868
Website: www.pccc.cc.nj.us

Burlington County College
County Road 530
Pemberton, NJ 08068-1599
609-894-4900
Website: www.bcc.edu

Ocean County College
College Drive
P.O. Box 2001
Toms River, NJ 08754-2001
732-255-0400
Website: www.ocean.cc.nj.us

Mercer County Community College
West Windsor Campus
1200 Old Trenton Road
Trenton, NJ 08690-1004
609-586-4800
Website: www.mccc.edu

Thomas Edison State College
101 West State Street
Trenton, NJ 08608-1176
609-292-6565
Website: www.tesc.edu

Essex County College, West Essex Campus
730 Bloomfield Avenue
West Caldwell, NJ 07006
201-403-2560
Website: www.essex.edu

NEW MEXICO

New Mexico State University at Alamogordo
P.O. Box 477
2400 North Scenic Drive
2400 Alamogordo, NM 88310
505-439-3600
Website: http://alamo.nmsu.edu

Albuquerque Technical Vocational Institute
525 Buena Vista Southeast
Albuquerque, NM 87106-4096
505-224-3000
Website: www.tvi.cc.nm.us

New Mexico State University-Carlsbad
1500 University Drive
Carlsbad, NM 88220-3509
505-234-9200
Website: http://cavern.nmsu.edu

Clovis Community College
417 Schepps Blvd.
Clovis, NM 88101-8381
505-769-2811
(will in future offer a program; contact college for details)
Website: www.clovis.cc.nm.us

New Mexico Junior College
5317 Lovington Highway
Hobbs, NM 88240-9123
800-657-6260
Website: www.nmjc.cc.nm.us

Dona Ana Branch Community College
MSC 3DA, P.O. Box 30001
New Mexico State University
Las Cruces, NM 88003-8001
505-527-7647
Website: http://dabcc-www.nmsu.edu

Eastern New Mexico University-Roswell
P.O. Box 6000
Roswell, NM 88201
505-624-7000
Website: www.roswell.enmu.edu

NEW YORK

Broome Community College
Upper Front Street
P.O. Box, NY 1017
Binghamton, NY 13902-1017
607-778-5000
Website: www.sunybroome.edu

Corning Community College
1 Academic Drive
Corning, NY 14830-3297
607-962-9220
Website: www.corning-cc.edu

Mercy College
555 Broadway
Dobbs Ferry, NY 10522-1189
800-MERCY-NY
Website: www.mercynet.edu

John Jay College of Criminal Justice/CUNY
Fire Science Division, Room 3529N
445 West 59th Street
New York, NY 10019
212-237-8092

Erie Community College-South Campus
4041 Southwestern Blvd.
Orchard Park, NY 14127-2199
716-851-1003
Website: www.ecc.edu

Monroe Community College
1000 East Henrietta Road
P.O. Box 9720
Rochester, NY 14623-5780
716-292-2000
Website: www.monroecc.edu

Schenectady County Community College
78 Washington Avenue
Schenectady, NY 12305-2294
518-381-1366
Website: www.sunysccc.edu

Rockland Community College
145 College Road
Suffern, NY 10901-3699
914-574-4237
Website: www.sunyrockland.edu

Onondaga Community College
4941 Onondaga Road
Syracuse, NY 13215
315-469-2201
Website: www.sunyocc.edu

NORTH CAROLINA
Central Piedmont Community College
P.O. Box 35009
Charlotte, NC 28235-5009
704-330-2722
Website: www.cpcc.cc.nc.us

Gaston College
201 Highway 321 South
Dallas, NC 28034
704-922-6214
Website: www.gastoncollege.org

Durham Technical Community College
1637 Lawson Street
Durham, NC 27703-5023
919-686-3300
Website: www.dtcc.cc.nc.us

Alamance Community College
P.O. Box 8000
Graham, NC 27253
336-578-2002
Website: www.alamance.cc.nc.us

Coastal Carolina Community College
444 Western Blvd.
Jacksonville, NC 28546-6877
910-455-1221
Website: www.coastalcarolina.org

Guilford Technical Community College
P.O. Box 309
Jamestown, NC 27282-0309
336-334-4822, ext. 5350
Website: www.technet.gtcc.cc.nc.us

Lenoir Community College
P.O. Box 188
Kinston, NC 28502-0188
252-527-6223
Website: www.lenoir.cc.nc.us

Davidson County Community College
P.O. Box 1287
Lexington, NC 27293-1287
336-249-8186
Website: www.davidson.cc.nc.us

Cape Fear Community College
411 North Front Street
Wilmington, NC 28401
910-251-5100
Website: www.cfcc.net

Wilson Technical Community College
P.O. Box 4305
Wilson, NC 27893-3310
252-291-1195
Website: www.wilsontech.cc.nc.us

OHIO
University of Akron
302 E. Buchtel Mall
Akron, OH 44325-2001
330-972-7100
Website: www.uakron.edu

Bowling Green State University
Continuing Education Division
40 College Park
Bowling Green, OH 43402
419-372-2531

Stark Technical College
6200 Frank Avenue NW
Canton, OH 44720-7299
330-966-5450
Website: www.stark.cc.oh.us

University of Cincinnati
College of Applied Science
100 East Central Park
Cincinnati, OH 45216
513-556-1100
Website: www.uc.edu

Cuyahoga Community College
Metropolitan Campus
2900 Community College Avenue
Cleveland, OH 44115
216-987-4030
Website: www.tri-c.cc.oh.us

Sinclair Community College
444 West 3rd Street
Dayton, OH 45402-1460
937-512-2500
Website: www.sinclair.edu

Delaware Junior Vocational School
1610 State Route 521
Delaware, OH 43015-9001
740-363-1993
Website: www.delawarejvs.org

Lorain County Community College
1005 Abbe Road North
Elyria, OH 44035-1691
800-995-LCCC
Website: www.lorainccc.edu

Lakeland Community College
7700 Clocktower Drive
Kirtland, OH 44094-5198
440-953-7000
Website: www.lakeland.cc.oh.us

Hocking Technical College
3301 Hocking Parkway
Nelsonville, OH 45764-9588
740-753-3591
Website: www.hocking.edu

Stark Technical College
6200 Frank Avenue NW
Canton, OH 44720
330-966-5450
Website: www.stark.cc.oh.us

Cuyahoga Community College
Western Campus
11000 Pleasant Valley Road
Parma, OH 44130-5199
216-987-5000
Website: www.tri-ccc.oh.us

Owens Community College-Toledo
P.O. Box 10000
Oregon Road
Toledo, OH 43699-1947
800-GO-OWENS
Website: www.owens.cc.oh.us

OKLAHOMA
Oklahoma State University
Technical Institute
900 North Portland Street
Oklahoma City, OK 73107-6120
405-945-3270

Oklahoma State University
219 Student Union
Stillwater, OK 74078
405-744-5358
Website: http://osu.okstate.edu

Tulsa Junior College
7505 West 41st Street
Tulsa, OK 74107
918-595-7000
Website: www.tulsa.cc.ok.us

OREGON
Clatsop Community College
1653 Jerome Avenue
Astoria, OR 97103-3698
503-325-0910
Website: www.clatsopcollege.com

Central Oregon College
2600 Northwest College Way
Bend, OR 97701-5998
503-383-7500
Website: www.cocc.edu

Southwestern Oregon Community College
1988 Newmark Avenue
Coos Bay, OR 97420-2912
800-962-2838
Website: www.southwestern.cc.or.us

Lane Community College
4000 East 30th Avenue
Eugene, OR 97405
541-747-4501
Website: http://lanecc.edu

Rogue Community College
Redwood Campus
3345 Redwood Highway
Grants Pass, OR 97527-9298
541-956-7500
Website: www.rogue.cc.or.us

Mt. Hood Community College
2600 SE Stark
Gresham, OR 97030-3300
503-491-6422
Website: www.mhcc.cc.or.us

Eastern Oregon State College
One University Boulevard
Division of Distance Education
La Grande, OR 97850-2899
541-962-3672
Website: www.eosc.osshe.edu

Western Oregon State College
345 North Monmouth Avenue
Monmouth, OR 97361
877-877-1593
Website: www.wou.edu

Portland Community College
1200 SW 49th Avenue
Portland, OR 97280-0990
503-977-4621
Website: www.pcc.edu

Umpqua Community College
1140 College Road
Roseburg, OR 97470
541-440-4600
Website: www.umpqua.cc.or.us

Chemeketa Community College
4000 Lancaster Drive NE
Salem, OR 97309-7070
503-399-5000
Website: www.chemek.cc.or.us

PENNSYLVANIA
Westmoreland County Community College
400 Armbrust Road
Youngwood, PA 15697
724-925-4000
Website: www.westmoreland.cc.pa.us

Montgomery County Community College
340 Dekalb Pike
Blue Bell, PA 19422-0796
215-641-6300
Website: www.mc3.edu

Harrisburg Area Community College
One HACC Drive
Harrisburg, PA 17110-2999
717-780-2300
Website: www.hacc.edu

Delaware County Community College
901 South Media Line Road
Media, PA 19063-1094
610-359-5050
Website: www.dccc.edu

Community College of Allegheny County
Boyce Campus
595 Beatty Road
Monroeville, PA 15146-1396
724-325-6614
Website: www.ccac.edu

Luzerne County Community College
1333 South Prospect Street
Nanticoke, PA 18634-3899
800-377-LCCC
Website: www.luzerne.edu

Community College of Philadelphia
1700 Spring Garden Street
Philadelphia, PA 19130-3991
215-751-8000
Website: www.ccp.cc.pa.us

Community College of Allegheny County
South Campus
1750 Clairton Road
West Mifflin, PA 15122-3097
412-469-4301
Website: www.cc.ac.edu

RHODE ISLAND
Providence College
School of Continuing Education
Providence, RI 02918
401-865-1000
Website: www.providence.edu

Community College of Rhode Island
Knight Campus
400 East Avenue
Warwick, RI 02886-1807
401-825-1000
Website: www.ccri.cc.ri.us

SOUTH CAROLINA
Greenville Technical College
P.O. Box 5616
Greenville, SC 29606-5616
803-250-8111
Website: www.greenvilletech.com

Midlands Technical College
Airport Campus
1260 Lexington Drive
West Columbia, SC 29170
803-738-8324
-or-
800-922-8038
Website: www.mid.tec.sc.us

SOUTH DAKOTA

Kilian Community College

224 North Phillips Avenue

Sioux Falls, SD 57104-6014

605-336-1711

Website: http://kcc.cc.sd.us

TENNESSEE

Chattanooga State Technical Community

College

4501 Amnicola Highway

Chattanooga, TN 37406-1018

423-697-4400

Website: www.cstcc.cc.tn.us

Volunteer State Community College

1480 Nashville Pike

Gallatin, TN 37066

615-230-3688

-or-

888-335-8722

Website: www.vscc.cc.tn.us

Roane State Community College

276 Patton Lane

Harriman, TN 37748

865-882-4523

-or-

800-345-9104

Website: www.rscc.cc.tn.us

University of Memphis

Memphis, TN 38152

901-678-2111

Website: www.memphis.edu

Southwest Tennessee Community College

(Formerly State Technical Institute at

Memphis)

5983 Macon Cove

Memphis, TN 38134

888-TECH-YES

-or-

901-382-TECH

-or-

901-333-4111

Website: www.stcc.cc.tn.us

Tennessee Technology Center

at Murfreesboro

1303 Old Fort Parkway

Murfreesboro, TN 37130

615-898-8010

Website: www.murfreesboro.tec.tn.us

TEXAS

Cisco Junior College

841 North Judge Ely Blvd.

Abeline, TX 79601

915-673-4567

Website: www.cisco.cc.tx.us

Texas Engineering Extension Service

Emergency Services Training Institute

John B. Connolly Building

301 Tarrow, TEEX

College Station, TX 77840-7896

Website: http://teexweb.tamu.edu

Amarillo College
P.O. Box 447
Amarillo, TX 79178-0001
806-371-5030
Website: www.uctx.edu

Trinity Valley Community College
100 Cardinal Drive
Athens, TX 75751
903-677-TVCC
Website: www.tvcc.cc.tx.us

Austin Community College
1212 Rio Grande
Austin, TX 78701
512-223-3030
Website: www.austin.cc.tx.us

Lamar Institute of Technology
P.O. Box 10043
Beaumont, TX 77710
409-880-8185
Website: http://theinstitute.lamar.edu

The University of Texas at Brownsville and
Texas Southmost College
80 Fort Brown Street
Brownsville, TX 78520
956-544-8200
Website: www.utb.edu

Blinn College, Bryan Campus
P.O. Box 6030
Bryan, TX 77805-6030
979-821-0220
Website: www.blinncol.edu

Del Mar College
101 Baldwin Boulevard
Corpus Christi, TX 78404-3897
361-698-1255
-or-
800-652-3357
Website: www.delmar.edu

Navarro College
3200 West 7th Avenue
Corsicano, TX 75110
903-874-6501
-or-
800-NAVARRO
Website: www.nav.cc.tx.us

El Paso Community College
P.O. Box 20500
El Paso, TX 79998-0500
915-831-2000
Website: www.epcc.edu

Fort Worth Fire Training Academy
1000 Calvert
Fort Worth, TX 76107
817-871-6875

Tarrant County College
Mary Owen Center
1500 Houston Street
Fort Worth, TX 76102-6599
817-515-5100
Website: www.tcjc.cc.tx.us

Galveston College
4015 Avenue Q
Galveston, TX 77550-7496
409-763-6551
(anticipated; contact school for details)
Website: www.gc.edu

Houston Community College
4310 Dunlaby
Houston, TX 77006
713-718-6111
Website: www.hccs.cc.tx.us

Kilgore College Fire Academy
100 Broadway
Kilgore, TX 75662
903-984-8662
Website: www.kilgore.cc.tx.us

Laredo Community College
West End Washington Street
Laredo, TX 78040-4395
210-721-5108
Website: www.laredo.cc.tx.us

South Plains College
1302 Main Street
Lubbock, TX 79401
806-747-0576
Website: www.spc.cc.tx.us

Collin County Community College
Central Park Campus
2200 West University Drive
P.O. Box 8001
McKinney, TX 75069-8001
214-548-6710
Website: www.ccccd.edu

Midland College
3600 North Garfield
Midland, TX 79705-6399
915-685-4500
Website: www.midland.cc.tx.us

Odessa College
201 West University
Odessa, TX 79764-7127
915-335-6432
Website: www.odessa.edu

San Jacinto College
Central Campus
P.O. Box 2007
8060 Spencer Highway
Pasadena, TX 77501-2007
281-476-1501
Website: www.sjcd.cc.tx.us

San Antonio College
1300 San Pedro Avenue
San Antonio, TX 78212
210-733-2000
Website: www.accd.edu

Tyler Junior College
P.O. Box 9020
Tyler, TX 75711-9020
903-510-2238
Website: www.tyler.cc.tx.us

UTAH

Utah Valley State College/Utah Fire and
Rescue Academy
3131 Mike Jense Parkway
Provo, UT 84601
801-764-7700
Website: www.uvsc.edu/ufra

VERMONT

Southeastern Vermont Career Education
Center (technical high school)
50 Fairground Road
Brattleboro, VT 05301
802-257-7335
Website: www.svcec.org

VIRGINIA

Northern Virginia Community College
8333 Little River Turnpike
Annandale, VA 22003-3796
703-323-3400
Website: www.nv.cc.va.us

Thomas Nelson Community College
P.O. Box 9407
Hampton, VA 23670
757-825-2700
Website: www.tncc.cc.va.us

J. Sargeant Reynolds Community College
108 East Grace Street
P.O. Box 85622
Richmond, VA 23285-5622
804-371-3029
Website: www.jsr.cc.va.us

Tidewater Community College
Virginia Beach Campus
1700 College Crescent
Virginia Beach, VA 23456
757-822-7255
Website: www.tc.cc.va.us

WASHINGTON

Bellevue Community College
3000 Landerholm Circle, S.E.
Bellevue, WA 98007-6484
206-641-2222
Website: www.bcc.ctc.edu

Olympic College
1600 Chester Avenue
Bremerton, WA 98337-1699
360-475-7723
Website: http://oc.ctc.edu

Lower Columbia College
1600 Maple
P.O. Box 3010
Longview, WA 98632-0310
360-577-2311
Website: http://lcc.ctc.edu

Edmonds Community College
20000 68th Ave West
Lynnwood, WA 98036-5999
425-640-1459
Website: www.edcc.edu

South Puget Sound Community College
2011 Moltman Road SW
Olympia, WA 98512
360-754-7711
Website: www.spscc.ctc.edu

Columbia Basin Community College
2600 North 20th Avenue
Pasco, WA 99301
509-547-0511
Website: www.cbc2.org

Spokane Community College
1810 N. Greene Street
Spokane, WA 99207-5399
509-533-7000
Website: www.scc.spokane.cc.wa.us

Bates Technical College
1101 South Yakima Avenue
Tacoma, WA 98405-4895
253-680-7000
Website: www.bates.ctc.edu

Pierce College at Fort Steilacoom
9401 Farwest Drive SW
Tacoma, WA 98498
253-964-6500
Website: www.pierce.ctc.edu

Wenatchee Valley College
1300 Fifth Street
Wenatchee, WA 98801
509-662-1651
Website: www.wvc.ctc.edu

Yakima Valley Community College
P.O. Box 22520
Yakima, WA 98907-2520
509-574-4600
Website: www.yvcc.cc.wa.us

WEST VIRGINIA
Shepherd College
P.O. Box 3210
Shepherdstown, WV 25443-3210
304-876-5000
Website: www.shepherd.wvnet.edu

WISCONSIN
Fox Valley Technical College
1825 N. Bluemound Drive
P.O. Box 2277
Appleton, WI 54912-2277
920-735-5600

Lakeshore Technical College
1290 North Avenue
Cleveland, WI 53015
888-468-6582
Website: www.gotoltc.com

Chippewa Valley Technical College
620 West Clairemont Avenue
Eau Claire, WI 54701
715-833-6200
-or-
800-547-2882
Website: www.chippewa.tec.wi.us

Moraine Park Technical College
P.O. Box 1940
235 North National Avenue
Fond du Lac, WI 54935-1940
414-922-8611
Website: www.moraine.tec.wi.us

Northeast Wisconsin Technical College
2740 West Mason Street
Green Bay, WI 53407-9042
715-735-9361
-or-
800-422-NWTC
Website: www.nwtconline.com

Blackhawk Technical College
6004 Prairie Road
P.O. Box 5009
Janesville, WI 53547
608-757-7713
Website: www.blackhawk.tec.wi.us

Madison Area Technical College
3550 Anderson Street
Madison, WI 53704
608-246-6100
-or-
800-322-6282
Website: www.madison.tec.wi.us

Wisconsin Indianhead Technical College
1019 South Knowles Avenue
New Richmond, WI 54017
715-246-6561

Milwaukee Area Technical College
South Campus
6665 South Howell Avenue
Oak Creek, WI 53154-1196
414-571-4500
Website: www.milwaukee.tec.wi.us

Gateway Technical College
1001 South Main Street
Racine, WI 53403
262-619-6232
Website: www.gateway.tec.wi.us

Mid-State Technical College
500 32nd Street North
Wisconsin Rapids, WI 54494
715-422-5300
Website: www.midstate.tec.wi.us

WYOMING

Casper College
125 College Drive
Casper, WY 82601
307-268-2110
Website: www.cc.whecn.edu

Laramie County Community College
1400 East College Drive
Cheyenne, WY 82007
307-778-LCCC
Website: www.lcc.whecn.edu

Participating Colleges/Universities: Open Learning Fire Service Program

Cogswell Polytechnical College
1175 Bordeaux Drive
Sunnyvale, CA 94089
408-541-0100
Contact: Linda R. Nascimento, Director
States served: AZ, CA, NV

University of Cincinnati
College of Applied Science
2220 Victory Parkway
Cincinnati, OH 45206
513-556-6583
Website: www.uc.edu/colleges/cas
Contact: Barbara Barkley
States served: FL, GA, IN, MI, MN, ND, OH, SD, WI

Memphis State University
University College
Johnson Hall, G-1
Memphis, TN 38152-6150
901-678-2716
Contact: Dr. Susanne Darnell, Associate Dean
Website: www.people.memphis.edu
States served: AL, AR, KY, LA, MS, TN, SC

Western Oregon University
Division of Extended Programs
Monmouth, OR 97361
503-838-8483
Website: www.wou.edu

Contact: Michelle Price
States served: AK, CO, HI, ID, MT, OR, UT, WA, WY

University of Maryland/
University College
Open Learning Program
University Blvd., at Adelphi Road
College Park, MD 20742
301-985-7722
Toll-free in MD: 800-888-UMUC
Toll-free in VA: 800-866-3726
Contact: JoAnne Hildebrand
States served: DE, MD, NJ, NC, DC, WV, VA

Western Illinois University
Educational Broadcasting and Independent Study
305 Memorial Hall
Macomb, Illinois 61455
309-298-2496
Contact: Dr. Joyce Nielsen, Associate Dean
Website: www.wiu.edu
States served: IL, IA, KS, MO, NE, NM, OK, TX

State University of New York (SUNY)
Empire State College
Center for Distance Learning
2 Union Avenue
Saratoga Springs, NY 12866
518-587-2100, ext. 300
Contact: Fire Service Coordinator
States served: CT, ME, MA, NH, NY, PA, RI, VT

Achieve Test Success With LearningExpress

Our acclaimed series of academic and other job related exam guides are the most sought after resources of their kind. Get the edge with the only exam guides to offer the features that test-takers have come to expect from LearningExpress—The Exclusive LearningExpress Advantage:

Easy to Use & Understand

- **THREE** Complete practice tests based on official exams
- Vital review of skills tested and hundreds of sample questions with full answers and explanations
- The exclusive LearningExpress Test Preparation System—must know exam information, test-taking strategies, customized study planners, tips on physical and mental preparation and more.

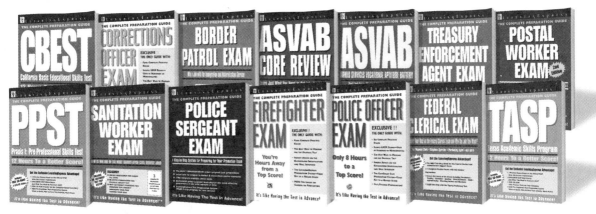